Rural Development, Income Distribution, and Fertility Decline

James E. Kocher is a Research Fellow in Demography in the Bureau of Resource Assessment and Land Use Planning at the University of Dar es Salaam, Tanzania, and a staff member of the Demographic Division of the Population Council. He is also a doctoral candidate in agricultural economics at Michigan State University.

RURAL DEVELOPMENT, INCOME DISTRIBUTION, AND FERTILITY DECLINE

JAMES E. KOCHER

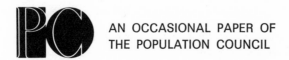

AN OCCASIONAL PAPER OF
THE POPULATION COUNCIL

THE POPULATION COUNCIL
245 Park Avenue
New York, New York 10017

The Population Council is an organization established in 1952 for scientific training and study in the field of population. It endeavors to advance knowledge in the broad field of population by fostering research, training, and technical consultation and assistance in the social and biomedical sciences.

The Council acknowledges, with thanks, the funds received from the Ford Foundation, the United Nations Fund for Population Activities, the United States Agency for International Development, the World Bank, and other donors for the publication program of the Population Council.

Distributed for The Population Council by
Key Book Service, Inc.
425 Asylum Street
Bridgeport, Connecticut 06610

Contents

List of Tables

chapter 4

Preface

Two development problems commanded center stage during the past decade. One was the food shortages of the mid-1960s; the second was the population explosion. Although these food shortages were followed by the green revolution breakthroughs, with few exceptions, neither fertility nor population growth rates have declined; in fact, in some countries the latter have increased as a result of the continuing decline in mortality. In a few important regions, the agricultural growth rate increased, and overall prospects are much brighter than they were ten years ago. Nevertheless, both agriculture and industry have been unable to absorb the rapidly growing labor force. As a consequence, many development specialists contend that the two central problems of the 1970s are unemployment and the continued population explosion.

The primary objective of this paper is to examine the process and components of rural development and their impact on fertility behavior and population growth in low-income countries. The central hypothesis is that the greater the extent to which the rural population is participating in development, the earlier and more rapid will be the decline in overall fertility and population growth rates.

Chapter 1 is an effort to clarify the meaning of "development." The demographic setting, both past and future, is presented in Chapter 2. Chapter 3 discusses some aspects of recent rural development in important areas of the low-income world. In Chapter 4 an attempt is made to substantiate the central hypothesis by examining the development and fertility experiences of several countries. The paper concludes with comments on research implications.

The main thesis of this paper can be summarized in the following set of propositions:

1. Populations in the low-income world are still largely rural—about 70 percent or more—and despite the high rates of urbanization and rural-to-urban migration that have been occurring and will almost certainly continue during the next few decades, these populations will remain predominately rural at least to the end of this century. By the year 2000, the rural population will still account for 50 to 60 percent of the total population in these countries.
2. In the absence of rural modernization, sustained overall fertility decline in rural areas *cannot* be anticipated.[1] Sustained fertility decline even in urban areas is problematic at best unless urban living conditions vastly improve within the next decade or two. I am aware of no evidence of sustained fertility decline—either spontaneous or induced through a family planning program—ever having taken place in the absence of significant socioeconomic development and modernization that considerably altered the lives of most of the population.[2]
3. It is quite possible for rural development to take place despite high fertility and rapid population growth. Considerable historical precedent exists; moreover, recent technological breakthroughs in agriculture provide convincing evidence that neither rapid population growth nor land scarcity nor traditional agriculture per se constitute insurmountable barriers to rural development. Rather, in most cases rural development in low-income countries is limited by the absence of adequate "modern" technology, particularly biological technology, as well as a host of political, economic, and other institutional obstacles. Development of the necessary biological technology requires resources outside the rural sector itself—usually national and international development resources organized to produce the necessary technology. Once available, if farmers have access to this technology along with the essential complement of "modern" agricultural inputs, and if a favorable institutional setting prevails, then rural development and modernization will usually take place, although it is a process that probably requires one or two decades to unfold.

---

[1] "Sustained overall fertility decline" means here a decline at the aggregate level that will continue until eventually reaching the low levels typical of contemporary high-income countries. For overall fertility decline to be sustained requires that an increasing proportion of the households in the population participate in the fertility decline.

[2] For a discussion of the meanings of "modernization," "development," and "growth," see Chapter 1.

4. The primary mechanism available for stimulating development is a dramatic increase in effective demand in the labor-intensive sectors through a more equal distribution of income. The potential is double-barreled in the sense that (a) effective demand can be increased in the aggregate, and (b) its composition can shift in a direction more favorable to domestically produced labor-intensive goods.

5. If the process of rural development gets underway as described above, and if it permeates the society so that most of the rural population experience improved living conditions and as a result find their lives progressively modernized, then associated with the "modernization" of their means of livelihood—that is, agriculture—will be the "modernization" of their attitudes toward family size. If contraceptive services are readily available, this will result in sustained overall fertility decline, although the fertility decline will probably lag somewhat behind the process of rural development.

Thus, it is this author's contention that fostering a pattern of development that results in a more equal distribution of income and other components of social and economic well-being (a) is desirable in and of itself; (b) will further stimulate the domestic production of both agricultural and non-agricultural goods by increasing domestic effective demand; (c) will lead to an earlier rather than a later spontaneous decline in overall fertility, which (d) will have beneficial feedback effects on human and physical capital formation and on the growth of effective demand, thereby further contributing to domestic socioeconomic growth and development.

It should be pointed out that economists have generally advocated a "growth-first-and-let-distribution-come-later" strategy, and that much of the development effort of the 1950s and 1960s was based on this approach.[3] It is argued in this paper that the recent development experience and future prognosis for low-income countries today is that a more equal distribution does not automatically follow rapid economic growth—or more precisely, if left to itself, distribution subsequently becomes more rather than less skewed. It follows from this argument that a further consequence is that overall fertility decline thus occurs later and slower rather than earlier and faster.

J. E. K.

May 1973
Dar es Salaam, Tanzania

---

[3] For example, according to both W. Arthur Lewis and Gustav Papanek, low-income countries must choose between growth and equality, and it is clear from their writings that both recommend growth: "An equal distribution of income is not compatible with economic growth" [Lewis, 1966, p. 96]. ". . . the inequalities in income contribute to the growth of the economy" [Papanek, 1967, p. 242].

Acknowledgments

The author is grateful to many people for their encouragement and helpful comments. He is particularly indebted to Carl Eicher, Tomas Frejka, Carl Gotsch, Hugo Hoogenboom, D. Gale Johnson, Bruce Johnston, Arleen Leibowitz, Arthur Mosher, Warren Robinson, Theodore W. Schultz, and David L. Sills.

The views expressed in this paper are not necessarily those of the Population Council.

Rural Development, Income Distribution, and Fertility Decline

chapter 1

The Meaning of Development

Recent Economic Growth

Since its beginning the science of economics or political economy has been preoccupied with trying to understand the process of economic growth. The conventional measure of economic growth is the level and rate of growth of aggregate or per capita national income (gross national or gross domestic product). Between 1950 and 1967, the average annual rate of growth of gross domestic product (GDP) was 4.8 percent in low-income countries as a group [Pearson et al., 1969].[1] This often is considered impressive since during comparable periods for high-income countries, GDP grew at rates averaging only 2–4 percent annually.[2] Yet from 1950 to 1970, population growth averaged nearly 2.5 percent per year in low-income areas. As a consequence,

---

[1] Throughout this paper the term "low-income" will be used when referring to the countries or regions of Asia (except Japan), Africa, and Latin America (except Argentina, and sometimes with the additional exceptions of Chile, Paraguay, and Uruguay, which together comprise temperate South America). The term is less value laden and therefore less objectionable than terms such as "underdeveloped," "less-developed," or "developing," but at the same time it captures a crucial distinction between these and the remaining· ("high-income") regions of the world.

[2] United Kingdom, 1790–1820, 2 percent; Germany, 1850–1880, 2.7 percent; United States, 1820–1850, 4 percent; Japan, 1876–1900, 4 percent [Pearson et al., 1969, p. 27].

per capita GDP growth rates were approximately the same in low-income countries as for comparable periods in high-income countries where—with the exception of North America—populations grew at only about 1 percent annually. Growth rates of low-income countries appear more disappointing when compared to growth rates of high-income countries during the period 1954–1958 to 1964–1968.

> In that period total product in both developed and less developed countries grew at about the same rate—4.6–4.7 percent per year, or almost 60 percent per decade. But population in the developed countries grew less than 1.2 percent per year, or less than 13 percent per decade; whereas that in the less developed countries grew at about 2.4 percent per year, or more than 27 percent per decade. As a result, per capital product in the less developed countries rose about 2.2 percent per year, whereas that in the developed countries grew almost 3.4 percent per year, and the relative disparity in per capita product between the two groups of countries widened somewhat, from a multiple of 10.7 to one of 12.0. [Kuznets, 1972, p. 185]

"Development" Defined

Economists have generally believed that if an economy is growing sufficiently rapidly (that is, about 5 percent annually),[3] the general socio-economic well-being (levels of living) of the whole population will improve, or at the very least its capacity for such improvements will be enhanced. Ranis summarizes the rationale underlying this expectation as follows:

> While there is by no means unanimity on how to define growth, it is convenient to adhere to the convention that real per capita national income or output represents the most reliable indicator of a system's economic achievement at any point in time and that any change in real per capita income over time connotes economic growth. Statesmen and philosophers have joined economists in recognizing that economic growth defined in this way represents the most objective indicator of a society's welfare. [Ranis, 1968, p. 409][4]

---

[3] Referring primarily to the 1960s, the Pearson Report stated, ". . . the growth record has been good. . . . The average total growth rate for seventy low-income countries since 1960 has been in line with the 5 per cent annual target established for the Decade and some twenty countries have maintained a growth rate of over 6 per cent per annum in the 1960's" [Pearson et al., 1969, p. 28].

[4] The following passage also implies that the term "standard of living" is synonymous with "per capita income" (and hence, a rise in per capita income automatically produces a corresponding rise in standard of living): "The United Nations has estimated that a one percent rise in population in the less developed countries may require from two to five percent rise in savings simply to provide the required capital to maintain a constant standard of living" [United Nations, 1951, p. 47].

In recent years, however, a number of economists have concluded that despite two decades of generally high rates of economic growth in the low-income world, social and economic welfare may have improved very little if at all because the distribution of benefits has apparently been highly unequal. Robert McNamara, president of the World Bank, observed in a speech to the United Nations Conference on Trade and Development that

> such evidence as is available suggests that even the developing countries which have registered significant gains in GNP growth rates are plagued with severely skewed income distribution patterns. [McNamara, 1972, p. 4]

There is growing evidence that in the low-income world "the inequalities seem to be increasing almost everywhere" [Myrdal, 1970, p. 452]. Data from India indicate that

> 40–50 percent of the total population has a per capita income below the official poverty line where malnutrition begins, and the per capita income of this group has declined over the last two decades while the average per capita income went up. [ul Haq, 1971, p. 5]

Moreover, much of the economic growth that has taken place in low-income countries to date could appropriately be called "perverse growth"; that is, it has undermined, rather than enhanced, the potential of the economy for long-term growth.[5] A leading Pakistani economist and architect of Pakistan's economic development strategy believes that

> the very institutions we created for promoting faster growth and capital accumulation later on frustrated all our attempts for better distribution and greater social justice. [ul Haq, 1971, p. 7]

As a consequence of these experiences, more and more economists are arguing that economic growth does not necessarily bring about economic development and that in many countries the prospects for a reduction of inequalities in the future are gloomy. Myrdal [1968, 1970] has forcefully argued for a more sensitive and humanitarian approach to development that would attack the causes of poverty. He regards increasing economic inequality as the most alarming trend in Asia. According to a leading international economist the questions to ask about development are:

---

[5] The characteristics of "perverse growth" include promotion of capital-intensive industrialization, usually in conjunction with institutionally overpriced wage labor (creating a "labor aristocracy") with consequent high propensities for imported consumer goods, highly-protected growth of import substitutes, underinvestment in the domestic capital-goods (consumption) sector, and the lack of internal agricultural incentives (in fact, frequently government-supported disincentives), thereby subjecting the agricultural sector to reliance on the "sluggish expansion of foreign demand" as the only stimulus to increased agricultural productivity [Arrighi and Saul, 1968, pp. 146–150].

> What has been happening to poverty? What has been happening to unemployment? What has been happening to inequality? If all three of these have declined from high levels, then beyond doubt this has been a period of development for the country concerned. If one or two of these central problems have been growing worse, especially if all three have, it would be strange to call the result "development," even if per capita income doubled. [Seers, 1970, p. 7]

Although there is not a clear consensus among economists as to the distinction between growth and development, throughout this paper the term "development" will mean the process of (1) a general improvement in levels of living, together with (2) decreasing inequality of income distribution, and (3) the capacity to sustain continuous improvements over time. The components of socioeconomic well-being are the substance of development. Inevitably there must be a certain arbitrariness in choosing the components to be included and their relative importance. A minimal, though not inclusive, set would consist of (a) income, (b) employment, (c) education, (d) health and nutrition, and (e) consumption, including food, housing, and such services as water supply, electricity, transportation, entertainment, police and fire protection, and so forth.[6]

Economic growth, as distinguished from development, can be defined as the long-term process of structural change in the methods of production resulting in rising aggregate and per capita income. Growth is clearly a necessary, though not sufficient, condition for socioeconomic development; as defined here, growth is a subset of development. Development could conceivably occur in the short run in the absence of economic growth. But the definition of "development" includes the capacity to sustain itself, and it is difficult to imagine sustained development without economic growth, particularly under circumstances of rapid population growth.

If an economy is to have future growth potential, current investments must be made—not only in the narrow sense of public and private funds transformed into capital equipment, but also investments in "people" that augment their future production and consumption capacities and opportunities. The latter must include investments in improving their health,

---

[6] In contrast to "development," by "modernization" I mean a transformation of life styles, which includes changes both in production and consumption activities and, more importantly, changes in values and attitudes that produce a societal environment conducive to rising levels of production and consumption. ". . . this transformation in perceiving and achieving wealth-oriented behavior entails nothing less than the ultimate reshaping and resharing of all social values, such as power, respect, rectitude, affection, well-being, skill, and enlightenment" [Lerner, 1968, p. 387]. It is conceivable, for example, that income, health, and educational attainment could all improve in the *absence* of modernization—that is, improvements could take place without any fundamental change in attitudes and values. However, it seems unlikely that modernization could take place in the absence of development.

skills, and education, and in moving them into more productive occupations and locations.

The Meaning of Rural Development

In Chapter 2 it is shown that by the end of this century the rural population in the low-income world will have increased by about 50 percent and will still comprise more than half of the total population. As in urban areas, rising individual and household incomes are an important aspect of rural development. Income is tied directly to employment or, more generally, to economic returns for work activities. Thus, rural development primarily implies generalized increases in (1) rural labor productivity resulting in growing incomes, and (2) rural employment opportunities sufficient to absorb the large numbers of new entrants into the rural labor force at continually rising levels of living.

Agricultural development is desirable for the simple reason that in most countries practically all of the rural population depend on agriculture for their livelihood. In addition, the capacity for both the urban and rural nonagricultural sectors to develop is effectively limited by productivity conditions in agriculture.[7] Nicholls [1969, p. 318] has emphasized the "almost universal importance of having a substantial and reliable agricultural surplus as the basis for launching and sustaining economic growth." As Johnston and his colleagues have argued in several important papers, agricultural productivity must increase to permit agriculture to make its essential "contributions" to overall development, including the net resource transfer to the nonagricultural sector that apparently has been a necessary condition for development in high-income countries [Johnston and Mellor, 1961; Johnston and Cownie, 1969; Johnston, 1970].

Kuznets has shown that in the United States during the period 1875–1945, while productivity in the nonagricultural sector was increasing by about 15 percent per decade, productivity in the agricultural sector was increasing even more rapidly. The ratio of productivity per worker in the agricultural sector to productivity per worker in the nonagricultural sector increased from about 0.4 to 0.7 during that seventy-year period. He concludes that

> a substantial rise in productivity of resources in the domestic agriculture sector is a condition of the large increase in overall productivity in modern economic growth. It is such a rise in productivity combined with the low income elasticity of demand for products of the agriculture sector, that accounts for the marked decline in the share of that sector in the total labor and capital used. [Kuznets, 1966, pp. 120–121]

---

[7] For a brief review of the role of agriculture in economic development in both the growth stage and dual-sector traditions of economic thought over the past 100 years, see Hayami and Ruttan, 1971, pp. 9–25.

Most post-World War II economic growth models and development strategies considered the agricultural or traditional sector as little more than the supplier of food and labor to the industrial sector, which was generally viewed as the sole source of growth and development. Retrospectively, perhaps the most damaging criticism of these models and strategies is that they failed to anticipate the tremendous growth of the rural population and the labor force that has occurred and will clearly continue. In addition, they were unduly optimistic about the capacity for urban-industrial strategies to generate new employment. In most countries, growth of urban wage employment has not even kept pace with the natural growth of the urban labor force. In Africa over the last decade or so, urban wage employment has typically been growing at less than 1.5 percent annually, while the urban population has generally been growing at over 6 percent annually [Frank, 1970]. The urban labor force has undoubtedly been growing even faster since about half of urban population growth is the result of rural-to-urban migration, which is made up predominantly of young job hunters. Experience has been equally dismal in most of Asia and Latin America. Urban-industrial strategies, as a consequence, doom most of the rural population—as well as a large portion of those who migrate to the cities—to socioeconomic stagnation.

Moreover, while it has long been recognized that the rural sector can serve general economic growth on the *supply* side (supplying food and labor and even savings to the expanding urban sector), it is becoming increasingly evident that it can play an important role by affecting *demand*. In low-income countries half or more of family income commonly is expended for food. Furthermore, usually a very large proportion of nonfood expenditures of low-income households is for domestically produced (or producible) labor-intensive goods. By utilizing cost-saving technologies and greater productive efficiency, the food supply can often be rapidly increased while its unit retail price substantially declines. The net result is usually that both food consumption and the amount of real income spent on nonfood items rises, which then stimulates further investment and employment in both rural and urban areas. Of course this presumes that the growth in real income on which this entire process depends is widely distributed so that most or all of the population experience rising incomes. If, however, only a small proportion benefits, the demand spin-off effects are likely to be minimal and distorted away from domestically produced employment-generating goods.

Finally, in rural areas one consequence of the "growth first" development strategies mentioned earlier has been the assignment of a low priority to land reform. In most of Asia and Latin America the highly unequal distribution of land ownership and tenancy rights continues to be a major cause of the highly skewed distribution of incomes and wealth [Myrdal, 1968, 1970; Dorner, 1971]. Although economists have often viewed land reform as inconsistent with the goal of maximizing growth in agricultural output [Adams,

1970; Petras and LaPorte, 1970; Nicholls, 1971], there are probably more historical examples of land reform *increasing* overall agricultural output than of its decreasing it [Dorner and Kanel, 1971].[8] It will be argued later that prevailing land tenure systems constitute a severe obstacle to rural development in many countries.

In summary, "economic development" has conventionally been defined as an adequate rate of growth of per capita income, and it has generally been assumed that if economic development so defined occurs, living conditions of all (or most) of the population will correspondingly improve. But we find, on the contrary, that despite generally satisfactory rates of growth in per capita income during the last two decades, living conditions in many parts of the world have not improved as expected and inequalities may have increased. True development is, instead, a process of sustained improvements in living conditions with ever greater equality in their distribution. Attention has been focused on rural development since in the low-income world most of the population live in rural areas and depend on agriculture for their livelihood. This condition will continue to exist for at least the next few decades as a result of rapid population growth and slow growth in nonagricultural employment. Finally, it has been suggested that considerable potential exists for agricultural development and that the agricultural sector can make an important contribution to overall economic development. However, in many parts of the low-income world, the prevailing land tenure system is a serious obstacle to agricultural development. These complex relationships are discussed more fully in Chapters 3 and 4.

---

[8] For a definition and fuller treatment of land reform, see Chapter 3.

chapter 2

Population Prospects

The "low-income world" could be characterized equally appropriately as the "high population growth rate world," or the "rural world." An examination of the growth prospects for total, urban, and rural populations up to the year 2000 in the low-income world can help put into perspective the crucial importance of an enlightened and progressive rural development strategy that will improve the living conditions of the growing rural population over the next generation. There is a very high probability that at the end of this century, nearly 60 percent of the people in the low-income world will still live in rural areas.

Population Growth

Changes in population size over time are the consequences of births minus deaths plus net migration. International migration is not very significant in most, especially large, low-income countries, although they do experience considerable internal migration. The most recently revised United Nations "medium" projection of crude birth and death rates and rates of natural increase to the year 2000 for the low-income world is presented in Table 2.1. While the birth rate is expected to decline by nearly one-third and the death rate by more than one-half over the next three decades, the

TABLE 2.1 Estimated and projected average annual crude rates, U.N. medium projection, low-income world, by decades, 1950–2000

Decade	Crude birth rate[a]	Crude death rate[a]	Crude rate of natural increase[a]
1950–1960	41	21	20 (2.0)
1960–1970	41	17	24 (2.4)
1970–1980	38	13	25 (2.5)
1980–1990	34	10	24 (2.4)
1990–2000	29	8	21 (2.1)

SOURCE: United Nations, 1971, Table 1, p. 3.

NOTE: The low-income world here includes all of Asia, Africa, and Latin America, with the exceptions of Japan and temperate South America.

[a] Per thousand per year. If net foreign migration is zero, the crude rate of natural increase is identical to the population growth rate, although the latter is usually given in percentage terms (as in the parentheses in column 4). A sustained population growth rate of 2.0 percent per year doubles the initial population in 35 years; a rate of 2.5 percent doubles the population in 28 years.

rate of population growth is expected to peak at 2.5 percent annually in the 1970–1980 decade and then decline by about one-sixth over the next two decades.[1]

Recent work in the utilization of population projection methodology enables an improved understanding of future lower limits to the size of populations as well as an idea of the range of possible population numbers lying ahead. Important in this context is the concept of the net reproduction rate (NRR). On the basis of current age-specific fertility and mortality rates, the NRR gives the number of daughters born per woman of childbearing age that will survive to the age of their mothers (provided the current demographic conditions do not change). "In other words, it is the number of daughters that could themselves become mothers. The NRR also approximates the rate at which the current generation of mothers is being replaced by a future generation of potential mothers" [Frejka, 1973, p. 30]. Thus, a fertility level corresponding to an NRR of 1.0 is sometimes called "replacement-level fertility" because it implies that one generation of females is

---

[1] The annual rate of population growth is conventionally given in percentage terms or, alternatively, as the rate of natural increase, which equals the crude birth rate (births per thousand population) minus the crude death rate. Although these accurately indicate the rate of population growth (provided net migration is zero) and approximately indicate fertility and mortality levels, the fertility schedule of women of childbearing ages (age-specific fertility rates) is considerably more informative about the average level of fertility of individuals; similarly with age-specific mortality. Standardized mortality rates and various demographic measures derived from age-specific fertility schedules provide more accurate inter- and intra-country comparisons of fertility and mortality levels than do crude rates alone.

replacing itself with a roughly identical number of females in the following generation.

Frejka has projected the population of the low-income world to the year 2000 and even to 2150 using five different assumptions about when an NRR of 1.0 will be achieved. Excluding Japan and temperate South America, the population of the low-income world in 1970 was 2.5 billion. If replacement-level fertility is attained some time between 1970–1975 and 2040–2045, the population of the low-income world in the year 2000 will be between 3.4 and 5.3 billion, and in 2050 between 4.1 and 11.6 billion.[2] However, the *probable* range for the year 2000 is narrower. In the low-income world taken as a whole, at the present time the gross reproduction rate (number of females born per woman of reproductive age) is about 2.8, while the NRR is 2.1 [Frejka, 1971, p. 10]. Multiplying by two, the average total number of births per woman during her reproductive life is about 5.6 (actually about 5.7 because of a male/female birth ratio greater than 1), while the average number surviving to adulthood is about 4.2. A net reproduction rate of 1.0 implies that about two children per woman are surviving to adulthood. Thus, under conditions of constant mortality, if the NRR declines from 2.1 to 1.0, the gross reproduction rate would decline from 2.8 to 1.3, implying that total births per woman of reproductive age must decline from 5.7 to about 2.7. If mortality conditions continue to improve, total births per woman must decline to below 2.7.

One can make a judgment about the likely lower limit of total population in the low-income world in the year 2000 based on what one is willing to accept as the earliest possible date by which women of reproductive age in the low-income world can, on the average, reach replacement level fertility of 2.7 (or less depending on mortality trends) children born—a decline from the current 5.7. Such an achievement requires a tremendous change in attitudes of parents as to their ideal or desired family size since at the present time desired family size—not simply number of births but number of surviving children—in the low-income world is generally in the range of 4 to 5 [Mauldin, Watson, and Noé, 1970]. A prerequisite to attainment of a net reproduction rate of 1 is that ideal number of children must decline from 4–5 to about 2. In addition, parents must have access to acceptable and effective means of contraception—a condition that is far from realization in most of the low-income world—so that, making some allowance for mortality conditions, parents can limit the average number of children born per family

---

[2] Frejka has demonstrated that it is inconceivable that the low-income world could attain zero population growth by the year 2000. "In most less developed countries fertility would have to decline very rapidly throughout the remainder of this century, and by the beginning of the twenty-first century an almost 1-child family would have to be the prevailing pattern. In India, for example, the average number of children per woman would have to be around 1.2 for about 20 years starting in the second half of the 1990s" [Frejka, 1973, p. 159].

to 2.7 or less. This of course cannot possibly come about in the next few years. In fact, *no* knowledgeable observer believes this can possibly happen by 1980–1985; a few believe this might come about by 2000–2005—one generation from now. If that is the case (Frejka's Projection Three), the *lower* limit of the low-income world population will be 4.5 billion by the year 2000 and 6.5 billion by 2050.[3] Similarly, unless fertility levels in the low-income world fail to decline at all in the next thirty years, in the year 2000 the low-income world could have 5.3 billion inhabitants and in 2050, 11.6 billion inhabitants (Frejka's Projection Five).

Regional Population Growth

Table 2.2 presents three alternative population projections for low-income regions for the period 1970–2000. The first two are Frejka's Projections Three and Five, made in 1972 and discussed earlier. The third is the United Nations "medium" projection made in the early 1960s. Although the underlying assumptions of each of the projections differ, the projected range in population size for the year 2000 is small. The population of Latin America is projected to increase between 95 and 125 percent from 1970 to 2000. For Africa the increase is between 80 and 123 percent; for Asia, 71 to 102 percent; and for all regions combined, 76 to 105 percent.

Urbanization

Although most of the attention given to population in low-income countries has concentrated on overall population growth, urbanization has in recent years become a major concern of many low-income countries. High rates of urban population growth and their associated crises of growing unemployment, inadequate housing and social services, and political unrest

---

[3] Because of the substantial population growth momentum inherent in the age structures and the current levels of fertility and mortality, the population in the low-income world would continue growing from 4.5 billion in the year 2000 to 6.5 billion in 2050 even if replacement-level fertility (net reproduction rate = 1) were to be attained during the period 2000–2005. That is, populations with high fertility have a very "young" age distribution. Typically, in low-income countries about 50 percent of the population is under twenty years of age, while typically in high-income countries only about 30 percent of the population is under twenty years of age. Thus, even if fertility in low-income countries should decline rapidly from its current high levels, the predominantly "young" age distribution that is the product of current high fertility would remain for some time. Those cohorts born during the period of high fertility must themselves pass through the childbearing ages—a process requiring nearly fifty years. Because they represent such a large proportion of the total population, they will continue to bear a large number of children and produce a growing population even if these cohorts of mothers themselves have quite low fertility.

TABLE 2.2   Population projections for low-income regions, 1970–2000

| | | Total population (millions) | | | Indices of growth | | |
| | | Frejka's projections | | United Nations | Frejka's projections | | United Nations |
Region	Year	Three	Five	projection[a]	Three	Five	projection[a]
Latin America	1970	283	283	285	100	100	100
	1980	367	375	380	130	133	133
	2000	540	626	640	195	221	225
Africa	1970	344	344	345	100	100	100
	1980	432	442	450	126	128	130
	2000	620	729	770	180	212	223
Asia	1970	2,040	2,040	2,005	100	100	100
	1980	2,543	2,593	2,445	125	127	122
	2000	3,544	4,115	3,435	174	202	171
Low-income world[b]	1970	2,667	2,667	2,635	100	100	100
	1980	3,342	3,410	3,275	125	128	124
	2000	4,704	5,470	4,845	176	205	184
East Asia	1970	940	940	910	100	100	100
	1980	1,130	1,146	1,040	120	154	114
	2000	1,485	1,646	1,285	158	175	141
South Asia	1970	1,100	1,100	1,095	100	100	100
	1980	1,413	1,447	1,405	128	132	128
	2000	2,079	2,469	2,150	189	224	196

SOURCES: Frejka, 1973; United Nations, 1969, Tables 36 and 37, p. 71.

[a] In 1970 the United Nations revised its "medium" projection, but regional figures have not yet been published [United Nations, 1971]. The revised "medium" projection for the entire low-income world is somewhat higher than the original "medium" projection presented above. Making the appropriate adjustments to include Japan and temperate South America so as to make the revised projections comparable with those above, the revised U.N. "medium" projection is much closer to Frejka's Projection Five than is the original U.N. "medium" projection. For example, the index of growth from 1970 to 2000 for the low-income world is 195 instead of 184 (last column above) as compared with 205 for Frejka's Projection Five and 176 for Frejka's Projection Three.

[b] Includes Japan and temperate South America.

are common to all low-income areas. A recent United Nations document begins:

> The most conspicuous feature of today's accelerated world population growth is its even greater rapidity of urbanization. In many periods in history, populations and cities have grown, but the tempo and dimensions of recent years have never been equalled. [United Nations, 1969a, p. 1]

Projecting rural and urban population growth is riskier and probably subject to more error than projecting total population growth since one must also project rural-to-urban migration, which commonly accounts for about half of total urban growth. There are no really satisfactory methods for estimating rural-to-urban migration for the more distant future, but the recent record can provide clues to possible rates. Table 2.3 gives what are

TABLE 2.3 Estimated rates of population growth: Total, urban, and rural, by regions, 1950–1970

Region	Period	Rates of population growth			Percent urban at beginning of period
		Total	Urban	Rural	
Latin America					
Middle America	1950–60	3.1	4.8	1.8	39.2
	1960–70	3.7	5.1	2.3	46.2
Caribbean	1950–60	2.2	3.1	1.7	35.2
	1960–70	2.4	3.5	1.7	38.5
Tropical South America	1950–60	3.1	5.4	1.6	35.8
	1960–70	2.8	4.6	1.1	44.7
Temperate South America	1950–60	1.9	2.8	0.3	59.1
	1960–70	1.9	2.7	0.3	65.0
Africa					
Northern	1950–60	2.4	4.3	1.7	24.6
	1960–70	2.6	4.2	1.8	29.6
Western	1950–60	3.4	6.9	2.9	10.6
	1960–70	3.1	6.2	2.5	14.7
Eastern	1950–60	2.5	5.5	2.2	5.6
	1960–70	2.5	5.3	2.2	7.5
Middle and southern	1950–60	1.8	7.7	1.3	6.4
	1960–70	2.0	4.9	1.5	11.6
South Africa	1950–60	2.5	3.9	1.5	39.1
	1960–70	2.3	3.5	1.2	44.9
Asia					
East[a]	1950–60	1.8	6.0	1.1	12.1
	1960–70	1.3	4.8	0.3	18.0
Southeast	1950–60	2.5	4.6	2.1	13.6
	1960–70	2.7	4.7	2.3	16.6
Southwest	1950–60	2.7	4.7	1.9	24.2
	1960–70	2.5	4.4	1.6	29.5
South central	1950–60	1.9	2.7	1.8	15.2
	1960–70	2.3	3.1	2.2	16.4

SOURCE: Adapted from Davis, 1969, Table C, pp. 113–138 and Table D, pp. 140–161.

[a] Japan is excluded.

perhaps the best available data estimating rates of both urban and rural population growth during the 1950s and 1960s. Generally, urban areas in Latin America grew at 3–5 percent annually; rates in Africa ranged from about 4–7 percent; and urban areas in Asia grew at something over 4 percent annually, with the exception of the south central region (India, Pakistan, and their neighbors), where urban areas grew 3 percent annually.

The most widely used projections of rural and urban population growth to the year 2000 were prepared by the United Nations using their "medium" projection (see the U.N. projection in Table 2.2). One must be aware that

TABLE 2.4   Estimated and projected total, rural, and urban populations, by regions, 1950–2000 (in millions)

Year	Latin America				Asia			
	Total	Rural	Urban	R–U[a]	Total	Rural	Urban	R–U[a]
1950	165	100	65	35	1,380	1,165	215	950
1960	215	110	105	5	1,650	1,315	335	980
1970	285	125	160	−35	2,005	1,525	480	1,045
1980	380	135	245	−110	2,445	1,770	675	1,095
1990	500	140	360	−220	2,935	1,990	945	1,045
2000	640	130	510	−380	3,435	2,165	1,270	895

	Africa				Total: low-income world[b]			
	Total	Rural	Urban	R–U[a]	Total	Rural	Urban	R–U[a]
1950	220	190	30	160	1,765	1,455	310	1,145
1960	270	220	50	170	2,135	1,695	440	1,195
1970	345	265	80	185	2,635	1,915	720	1,240
1980	450	325	125	200	3,275	2,230	1,045	1,270
1990	585	390	195	195	4,020	2,520	1,500	1,130
2000	770	470	300	170	4,845	2,765	2,080	810

	East Asia				South Asia			
	Total	Rural	Urban	R–U[a]	Total	Rural	Urban	R–U[a]
1950	685	580	105	475	695	585	110	475
1960	795	615	180	435	855	700	155	545
1970	910	665	245	420	1,095	860	235	625
1980	1,040	715	325	390	1,405	1,055	350	705
1990	1,170	750	420	330	1,765	1,240	525	715
2000	1,285	765	520	245	2,150	1,400	750	650

SOURCE: Adapted from United Nations, 1969, Tables 23, 35, 36, and 37, pp. 48, 50, and 71.

[a] R–U = Rural *minus* Urban; it indicates the extent to which the rural population exceeds the urban population in absolute numbers.

[b] Includes Japan and temperate South America.

actual rural and urban population futures may differ from these projections. Nevertheless, these projections—presented in Table 2.4—represent the best available estimate of future likelihoods based on existing knowledge. Table 2.5 gives the index numbers of implied total, rural, and urban population growth (1950 = 100). The numbers in parentheses indicate the implied rates of annual growth. Table 2.6 presents the implied percentages of rural and urban distributions to the year 2000. Note that over the fifty-year period 1950–2000, the urban population is expected to increase by a multiple of ten in Africa, eight in Latin America, six in Asia, and almost seven in the low-income world as a whole (Table 2.5).

TABLE 2.5 Indices of estimated and projected growth of total, rural, and urban populations, by regions, 1950–2000

	Latin America			Asia		
Year	Total	Rural	Urban	Total	Rural	Urban
1950	100	100	100	100	100	100
1960	130(2.6)	110(0.9)	162(4.8)	120(1.8)	113(1.2)	156(4.4)
1970	173(2.9)	125(1.2)	246(4.2)	145(1.9)	131(1.5)	223(3.6)
1980	230(2.8)	135(0.7)	377(4.3)	177(2.0)	152(1.5)	314(3.4)
1990	303(2.8)	140(0.4)	554(3.8)	213(1.9)	171(1.2)	440(3.4)
2000	388(2.5)	130(−0.7)	785(3.5)	249(1.6)	186(0.8)	591(3.0)

	Africa			Low-income world		
	Total	Rural	Urban	Total	Rural	Urban
1950	100	100	100	100	100	100
1960	123(2.1)	116(1.5)	160(4.7)	121(1.9)	116(1.5)	142(3.5)
1970	157(2.4)	139(1.8)	267(5.1)	149(2.1)	132(1.3)	232(4.9)
1980	205(2.7)	171(2.1)	417(4.5)	186(2.2)	153(1.5)	337(3.7)
1990	266(2.6)	205(1.8)	650(4.4)	228(2.0)	173(1.2)	484(3.6)
2000	350(2.7)	247(1.9)	1,000(4.3)	275(1.9)	190(0.9)	672(3.3)

	East Asia			South Asia		
	Total	Rural	Urban	Total	Rural	Urban
1950	100	100	100	100	100	100
1960	116(1.5)	106(0.6)	171(5.4)	123(2.1)	120(1.8)	141(3.4)
1970	133(1.4)	115(0.8)	233(3.1)	158(2.5)	147(2.0)	214(5.7)
1980	152(1.3)	123(0.7)	310(2.9)	202(2.5)	180(2.0)	318(4.0)
1990	171(1.2)	129(0.5)	400(2.5)	254(2.3)	212(1.6)	477(4.1)
2000	188(0.9)	132(0.2)	495(2.1)	309(2.0)	239(1.2)	682(3.6)

SOURCE: Based on Table 2.4.

NOTE: Numbers in parentheses are implied rates of annual increase during the preceding decade.

TABLE 2.6   Rural-urban populations: Percentage distributions, by regions, 1950–2000

Year	Latin America		Asia		Africa	
	Rural	Urban	Rural	Urban	Rural	Urban
1950	61	39	84	16	86	14
1960	51	49	80	20	81	19
1970	44	56	76	24	77	23
1980	36	64	72	28	72	28
1990	28	72	68	32	67	33
2000	20	80	63	37	61	39

Year	Low Income world		East Asia		South Asia	
	Rural	Urban	Rural	Urban	Rural	Urban
1950	82	18	85	15	84	16
1960	79	21	77	23	82	18
1970	73	27	73	27	79	21
1980	68	32	69	31	75	25
1990	63	37	64	36	70	30
2000	57	43	60	40	65	35

SOURCE: Adapted from United Nations, 1969, Tables 23, 35, 36, and 37, pp. 48, 50, and 71.

Rural Population Growth

Despite the widespread trend to urbanization, rural populations continue to grow. During the 1950–1970 period, rural populations in the low-income world grew at 1–2 percent annually; more than half a billion additional people were added to the rural world. By the year 2000, total rural population is expected to be nearly double its 1950 size. In the thirty-year period from 1970 to 2000, the rural population is expected to increase by a few percent in Latin America, by 15 percent in East Asia, by over 60 percent in South Asia, by about 80 percent in Africa, and by nearly 50 percent for the low-income world as a whole. While the urban population might increase by 1.4 billion from 1970 to 2000, the rural population is expected to grow by almost a billion and still comprise between half and two-thirds of the total population of the low-income world. If development policies are intended to improve the well-being of all the people, they must be designed for this rural majority as well as the mushrooming urban dwellers.

chapter 3

Rural Development

the record

Rural development essentially means continuous and self-sustaining improvements in the levels of living of rural people. Agricultural development differs only in that it is concerned specifically with a rapid growth in agricultural production per se as well as a fairly equal distribution of the benefits of development among the agricultural population. Since in most low-income countries nearly all rural people are agriculturalists, there is usually very little difference between the context of rural and agricultural development.

This chapter will review the current state of agricultural growth and development in the low-income world and discuss recent trends and future prospects. Chapter 4 will analyze the relationships between rural development and fertility decline, primarily by examining some of the more important and better-documented instances of rural development and fertility decline.

The Food Situation in Low-Income Countries

During the 1960s the "food" problem was considered a major element of the "population" problem because it was feared that food production could not keep pace with population growth. In the middle 1960s the sense of crisis heightened as the monsoons on the Indian subcontinent failed and food production first stagnated, then declined. India, with a population only slightly smaller than that of Africa and Latin America combined, averted large-scale famine only by massive shipments of wheat from the United States. During this period, 40 percent of the United States wheat crop was annually being shipped abroad as food aid [Brown, 1970, pp. 170–171]. By January 1968 India alone had received $3.3 billion in food aid under the PL 480 program (also called the Food for Peace Program). From 1954 through 1967, United States food aid to low-income countries totaled $17.2 billion; the annual average for the mid-1960s was $1.5 billion [Cochrane, 1969, p. 134].

Total "demand" for food (how much food people are prepared to buy at prevailing price and income levels) is a function of both population growth—the "population effect"—plus the additional demand that results from rising incomes—the "income effect." People with low incomes have a highly elastic demand for food. That is, they spend a large part of additional income for food, typically 60–80 percent of any income gains [Stevens, 1965]. Thus, if per capita incomes are rising, demand for food will be increasing more rapidly than the rate of population growth. The Food and Agricultural Organization (FAO) recently estimated that in order to meet world requirements, food production must increase at an average annual rate of 3.9 percent from 1962 to 1985; the actual rate of increase from 1960 to 1966 was only 2.4 percent [FAO, 1970, vol. I, pp. 13–14].

Despite these rather ominous food production figures, despite preoccupation in the 1960s with averting mass starvation, and despite the failure of the rate of population growth to decline in most of the low-income world and thereby ease the burden on agriculture, in the late 1960s the general consensus concerning the capability of low-income countries of the world to feed themselves in the near future changed from pessimistic to optimistic. This is reflected in the writings of Lester Brown. As an international agricultural economist with the U.S. Department of Agriculture, Brown [1963] argued that prospects for the low-income world producing enough food for its own needs were gloomy. Some major regions, particularly India, might well become permanently dependent on food imports from the United States. The need for food aid would increase dramatically in the years ahead. In a later book, Brown [1970] reversed his earlier judgment and concluded that prospects were quite good that the low-income world would be able to feed itself in the 1970s and 1980s. He argued that United States food aid could and *should* cease, lest it depress production incentives for farmers in low-income countries. According to Brown [1968], a new agricultural era began in about 1967, at which time the low-income world acquired the capability of increasing food production more rapidly than population. Despite this new capability, however, 1972 food production fell short in some major parts of the world—notably India, Bangladesh, U.S.S.R., and large parts of Southeast Asia—again demonstrating that the precarious balance between population growth and food supplies is in constant danger of being upset, and that no one really knows the future of the world food supply.

The Green Revolution: The Record and the Prospects

This new era of hope is the result of the so-called green revolution, a term that encompasses both biological and socioeconomic developments. Agricultural scientists have developed new crop varieties, particularly of wheat and rice, which—when properly complemented with fertilizer, water, pest and disease control agents, and other improved farming practices—have the potential for outyielding the best traditional varieties by at least two to three times.[1] As a consequence, the possibilities for rural socioeconomic change are considerable; indeed, some change has already taken place.

The present green revolution had its beginnings in the 1940s in Mexico. Supported by the Rockefeller Foundation, scientists developed varieties of wheat with yield potentials vastly superior to indigenous varieties. By 1957, 1.8 million acres of wheat in Mexico—90 percent of the total—were planted to high-yielding varieties [Dalrymple, 1972, p. 3]. In the early 1960s a rice breeding program was begun at the International Rice Research Institute in the Philippines. The first year of extensive plantings in Asia of both new rice varieties and Mexican wheat varieties was 1965–1966, when about 40,000 acres were planted. Five years later, in 1970–1971, over 50 million acres in Asia were planted to high-yielding varieties, about half to wheat and half to rice (see Table 3.1).

More comprehensive and up-to-date data are available on total area planted or harvested than on yields of new high-yielding varieties. Table 3.1 presents data on harvesting or planting for the countries of Asia and North Africa—the major regions into which the new varieties have been introduced. In 1970–1971, of the total wheat land, one-half in Pakistan and one-third in India were planted to new varieties. The spread of high-yielding varieties of rice was slowed initially by inadequate water supply and control structures, but in the two years from 1968–1969 to 1970–1971 acreage planted more than doubled. Half the rice area in the Philippines and two-fifths in Pakistan were planted to new varieties of rice. The most rapid spread of high-yielding wheat occurred from 1966–1967 to 1968–1969, when acreage planted increased from 1.5 million to 19.8 million. By 1970–1971 over 20 percent of the total wheat land in Asia and North Africa and about 13 percent of the rice land in Asia were planted to high-yielding varieties.

Although comparable data are not available, it is estimated that in Latin America improved varieties of rice were planted on 750,000 to 1,000,000 acres in 1970–1971, primarily in Cuba, Costa Rica, Mexico, Nicaragua,

---

[1] Data for India, Pakistan, and Turkey indicate that semidwarf (high-yielding) varieties of wheat outyielded local (traditional) varieties by the following ratios in 1970: India, 3.6 to 1; Pakistan, 1.8 to 1; Turkey, 3.3 to 1 [Tsu, 1971, pp. 13, 17, 21]. The acreages to which these yield data refer are approximately the same as those given in Table 3.1.

TABLE 3.1 Use of high-yielding varieties of wheat and rice in Asia and North Africa: Acres planted or harvested, 1965–1966 to 1970–1971 (in thousands)

Country	1965–66	1966–67	1967–68	1968–69	1969–70	1970–71	HYV as percent of total: 1970–71[a]
HIGH-YIELDING WHEAT							
South Asia							
Afghanistan	—	4.5	54.4	301.5	360.8	574.3	7.8
Bangladesh	—	—	—	20.0	22.0	24.0	7.7
India	7.4	1,270.0	7,270.0	11,844.0	12,133.0	14,599.0	32.9
Nepal	3.5	16.2	61.3	132.9	186.6	242.7	25.3
Pakistan	12.0	250.0	2,365.0	5,900.0	6,626.0	7,288.0	48.7
West Asia							
Iran	—	—	—	25.0	222.4	321.2	3.1
Iraq	—	—	15.8	103.0	482.4	309.0	6.2
Jordan	—	—	—	0.2	0.3	0.3	0.1
Lebanon	—	—	—	0.7	6.0	8.6	5.7
Syria	—	—	—	—	—	94.0	10.1
Turkey	—	1.5	420.0	1,444.0	1,343.0	1,184.0	5.8
North Africa							
Algeria	—	—	—	—	12.4	346.0	4.7
Morocco	—	—	0.5	12.1	24.7	49.4	4.0
Tunisia	—	—	2.0	32.0	131.0	255.0	14.0
Total	22.9	1,542.2	10,189.0	19,815.4	21,550.6	25,255.5	21.9

HIGH-YIELDING RICE

South Asia								
Bangladesh	—	0.5	166.0	381.5	651.7	1,137.0	3.3
India	17.7	2,195.0	4,408.0	6,625.0	10,729.0	13,593.0	14.7
Nepal	—	—	—	105.1	123.0	167.6	5.8
Pakistan	—	0.2	10.0	761.0	1,239.0	1,548.0	41.7
Sri Lanka	—	—	—	17.2	65.1	73.0	4.5
East Asia							
Burma	—	—	8.5	412.4	355.9	496.3	4.0
Indonesia	—	—	—	488.4	1,854.0	2,303.4	11.3
South Korea	—	—	—	—	—	7.2	—
Laos	—	0.9	3.0	5.0	4.9	132.5	7.0
Malaysia	—	104.5	157.0	224.7	238.1	327.1	24.5
Philippines	—	204.1	1,733.4	2,500.0	3,345.6	3,686.1	50.3
Thailand	—	—	—	—	—	400.0	2.1
South Vietnam	—	—	1.2	100.0	498.0	1,240.3	19.3
Total	17.7	2,505.2	6,487.1	11,620.3	19,104.3	25,293.5	13.0
Grand Total	40.6	4,047.4	16,676.1	31,435.7	40,654.9	50,549.0	16.3

SOURCE: Dalrymple, 1972, pp. 48–51.

ᵃ Estimated area devoted to high-yielding varieties as a percent of the area devoted to all varieties of the same crop; South Korea is excluded for lack of data.

— = High-yielding varieties not yet in use.

Colombia, Ecuador, Guyana, and Venezuela. In 1971, 90 percent of Egypt's total wheat acreage of 1.35 million acres was planted to an improved local variety with about the same yield per acre as that of high-yielding varieties in Mexico [Dalrymple, 1972, pp. 11 and 28].

Since the mid-1960s, food production has generally increased rapidly in the green revolution areas. After a record harvest in India of 89 million metric tons in 1964–1965, output fell to 72 and 74 million tons the next two years [Abel, 1971, p. 36]. But with increasing use of new varieties and better weather, production reached 96 million tons in 1967–1968, 100 million in 1969–1970, 108 million in 1970–1971, and 113 million in 1971–1972 [Abel, 1971, p. 36; Rangan, 1972]. In 1971 India attained self-sufficiency in rice production after years as a major world importer. The experiences of most other Asian countries have been similar [Sterba, 1972]. Development of improved varieties continues in several major research centers around the world, not only in wheat and rice but other food crops as well. For example, a hybrid maize was introduced into Kenya in 1964; by 1968 production had tripled to 3.5 million tons [Eicher and Zalla, 1971]. It is widely expected that the green revolution will reach many more of the world's low-income countries within this decade.

These new agricultural developments have been interpreted as providing a respite of fifteen years or more from the Malthusian disaster frequently predicted for the 1970s.[2] Norman Borlaug, often called the "father of the green revolution," and a recipient of the Nobel Peace Prize for his contributions as a plant breeder, has written:

> The green revolution has won a temporary success in man's war against hunger and deprivation; it has given man a breathing space. If fully implemented, the revolution can provide sufficient food for sustenance during the next three decades. But the frightening power of human reproduction must also be curbed; otherwise, the success of the green revolution will be ephemeral only. [Borlaug, 1971, p. 8]

Other development specialists worry that "second generation" problems threaten to undo many of the production gains. More than three years ago Wharton [1969] identified a set of rural bottlenecks likely to limit the spread of green revolution technology, including (1) limited availability of irrigated land, (2) inadequate marketing, transportation, and storage facilities, (3) inadequate farming skills, and (4) institutional patterns that disadvantage small farmers and tenants. Recent experience has shown many of Wharton's concerns to be well founded. Progress reports of the past two years have consistently struck two themes. First, although there have been occasional setbacks, overall growth in output is increasing rapidly—about 3–4 percent

---

[2] For example, see Paddock and Paddock, 1967, and Ehrlich, 1968.

annually—but not as spectacularly as some had predicted. Second, this growth in output is being accompanied by serious social and economic side effects.

Part of the reason for the unequal distribution of the green revolution's benefits is that, while the package of new inputs is theoretically neutral to scale, in practice as farm size increases, the proportion of farmers adopting the new technologies usually also increases [Schulter, 1971; Abel, 1971, pp. 44–46]. Typically, only larger farmers have the political power or sophisticated agricultural knowledge to secure financing (credit) and with it the seeds, fertilizer, water pumps, and so on, which are often in limited supply. Small farmers are more likely to be left out; tenant farmers may be forced off the land; small landowners may be bought out by the larger and wealthier ones.

Rochin [1971] reviewed the results of five separate studies carried out in (West) Pakistan during 1969 and 1970. Based on this review, he was not able to state categorically that farmers with small holdings have participated less in the green revolution. Nevertheless, he reports a tendency for farmers with larger holdings to have had greater access to credit and water and greater contact with extension workers; these farmers were likely to have received the economic advantage of being among the first to have used the new varieties. Gotsch documents the differential access to the new technologies—particularly tubewells—that permit Pakistan's larger farmers to acquire the appropriate inputs while smaller farmers either do without or use water and other costly inputs at suboptimal levels.

> The conclusion is therefore inescapable that so long as small farmers are finding it difficult to gain access to services, the private tubewell will be a source of increasing income inequity in Pakistan. [Gotsch, 1972, p. 335]

He contrasts this with the Comilla community in Bangladesh where a farmers' cooperative has succeeded in providing adequate water to farmers with all sizes of holdings. He concludes that

> the wide-spread participation of the small and middle peasant group in the Comilla program will tend to maintain the relatively equalitarian distribution of income that currently exists. [pp. 335–336]

Unfortunately, even the Comilla experience has its darker side. Very small farmers and landless laborers have generally not participated in the cooperative movement and have therefore been excluded from the yield gains made possible by the cooperative. However, since the new seed-fertilizer-water package is labor-intensive and requires 50–70 percent more labor per acre, their relative disadvantage has been partially offset by an increased demand for labor resulting from the cooperative-financed large increases in acreage brought under winter cropping.

Another important consequence of rapidly rising agricultural output is that countries that have traditionally had food deficits will have to readjust their price structure. Prices for basic food goods have typically borne little resemblance to world prices. Support prices for rice have recently ranged from US$36 per ton in Burma to $93 in the Philippines, and $123 in Ecuador. Wheat price per ton has been $64 in Mexico, $87 in Turkey, and $101 in India [Falcon, 1970, p. 702].

This leads to a consideration of perhaps the single most disturbing consequence of the green revolution: the likelihood that in many regions of these countries levels of living, and even food production, will decline. This will be the result of the highly unequal regional agricultural growth and development that will undoubtedly take place in the years ahead. Cleaver [1972, p. 91] calls this one of the major contradictions of the green revolution. Lele and Mellor write:

> The explosive widening of regional income disparities is one of the most intractable consequences of the "green revolution." It is the poorer class in the backward regions who suffer the greatest inequity in economic development. [Lele and Mellor, 1972, p. 28]

Regional disparities will come about because first, the characteristics of the new agricultural technologies are more suited to some regions (for example, those with controlled water supplies) than to others; consequently, agricultural output will expand rapidly in areas well suited to the new technologies while stagnating in others. Second, as production of food crops expands under conditions in which prices are artificially supported—as in most countries—at levels far above world prices, governments will have to adjust their support prices downward or subsidize huge surpluses, which would create an intolerable financial burden. Declining prices of primary foodstuffs will have substantial benefits to the country as a whole. They will release some financial resources—both private and public—from expenditure for food and permit them to be used to provide more nonfood consumption and/or savings and investment, while at the same time permitting improved food consumption and nutrition for people who buy their food. However, for those farmers in regions that cannot exploit the new technologies—and for those farmers in green revolution regions who do not exploit them—declining commodity prices at the farm level will mean declining incomes, deteriorating living conditions, and probably substantial socioeconomic dislocation and out-migration from these regions. This unfortunate side effect of agricultural progress is not without ample historic precedent as attested to by Appalachia and other regions within the United States, southern Italy, southern Mexico, and similar regions in other countries. Many observers predict that for a large proportion of India's rural small landowners and landless people, the net effect of all these agricultural changes will be further impoverishment, rising unemployment, and massive migration to already crowded cities.

In sum, recent agricultural breakthroughs offer real potential for continued high rates of increase in food production—perhaps 3.5–4 percent annually—for the next decade or two. This is certainly superior to the 2.5 percent average of the last two decades, and it provides a real opportunity for meaningful development of rural areas with substantial development benefits to nonagricultural sectors. It is also about the rate of growth in agricultural output that the Food and Agricultural Organization calculated would be required to meet increasing food demands for the next fifteen years. But it is clear that for those regions of the low-income world where new biological technologies are now or soon will be available, the extent to which their full potential will be exploited depends on the willingness of governments to provide a suitable economic and institutional structure. For example, it has been argued that in the Philippines the government is largely to blame for recent agricultural production shortfalls. Land reform and programs to provide credit, seeds, fertilizers, and pesticides have all been victims of vested interests, politics, and corruption [Starner, 1972]. As a consequence, much of the green revolution potential in the Philippines has been wasted.

Similarly, the *distributional* consequences of green revolution breakthroughs depend largely on economic and institutional circumstances. The outcome does not appear to be predetermined; nevertheless, there is considerable reason for alarm. This issue probes more directly at "development" per se, and a more extensive discussion follows. Distributional issues, particularly employment and income distribution, are looming as the major development focus of the 1970s.

Employment

While rural development is the primary focus of this paper, discussions of some aspects of development do not lend themselves to an easy separation of rural from nonrural, either because of the nature of the interrelationships between the two sectors or data limitations or both. To a considerable extent this is true for both employment and income distribution. Nevertheless, employment and income distribution are among the most important components of development and are key determinants of the distribution of development benefits for rural and urban populations as well as for societies as a whole. The following discussion of employment and that of income distribution in the subsequent section will focus—to the extent that data limitations permit—first on the overall economy or society and then on the rural sector in particular.

The emergence of unemployment as a central concern of economic development is indicated in part by the amount of scholarly attention recently paid to the topic. Within the last three years the Organization for Economic Cooperation and Development (OECD) has published a major review [Turnham, 1971a]; the International Labour Organization (ILO) has produced several monographs on employment and development and major country studies of Colombia, Sri Lanka (formerly Ceylon), and Kenya [ILO, 1970, 1971, 1972]; three monographs have focused specifically on agricultural development [Eicher et al., 1970; Shaw, 1970; and Yudelman et al., 1971]; numerous international and regional conferences have been held, and hundreds of papers have been published.

Levels of Unemployment in the Low-Income World

In most countries the urban labor force is growing at about 2 percent or more annually from natural increase alone. Many urban centers are growing at an additional 2–3 percent annually as a result of migration. Since migrants are predominantly young workers aged fifteen to thirty, the urban labor force is usually growing still faster. Thus, as a consequence of both natural increase and migration, the urban labor force in most low-income countries is growing at 5–10 percent annually. Urban wage employment opportunities have generally been increasing very slowly if at all. For example, from 1925 to 1960, about 23 million people were added to the urban labor force in Latin America. Only 5 million were absorbed in manufacturing. The percentage of the nonagricultural labor force employed in manufacturing declined from 35.4 to 27.1 [Thiesenhusen, 1971a]. In five of the ten anglophone African countries for which data are available, nonagricultural employment grew at less than 1.0 percent annually from the mid-1950s to the mid-1960s [Frank, 1970, pp. 5–8]. In only two of the ten—Ghana and Sierra Leone—did it grow at 3 percent or more. At the same time, urban populations were growing at up to 10 percent (or more) annually, and the urban labor force was growing even more rapidly. Still more ominous, because fertility has generally remained high over the last two decades while mortality, and particularly infant mortality, has been falling rapidly, the cohorts aged 0–15 are now growing at rates even higher than those of the overall population. Thus, over the next two decades the additions to the labor force will be even larger than current population growth rates would lead us to expect.

Although evidence generally indicates that the urban labor force is growing rapidly while the aggregate demand for labor is increasing only slowly, in most countries the actual level of urban unemployment is not known. There is not even a general consensus among economists on how to define unemployment. But available evidence indicates that in Latin America at least 10–15 percent of the labor force in urban areas are openly unemployed [Beller, 1970]. Todaro [1971] and Frank [1970] have statistics showing that from 15–25 percent of the urban labor force in some African cities are unemployed. Turnham [1971a, pp. 48–50] presents data on recent levels of urban unemployment for several low-income countries that show male unemployment rates ranging up to 18.4 percent in Guyana and 25.9 percent in Alger, Algeria. Without exception, unemployment rates are markedly higher among those aged fifteen to twenty-four, in some cases more than double the overall rates. In Alger, 41 percent in this younger age group are reported as unemployed while the percentages are 36 in both Guyana and Sri Lanka.

The scanty available evidence indicates that open unemployment—especially seasonal—also exists in some rural areas, but its extent is unknown. During the 1950s and 1960s, there was considerable disagreement among economists about the existence and extent of rural underutilization of labor. In 1951 a United Nations study concluded that up to one-third of the rural labor force in many regions of Asia was redundant [United Nations, 1951]. On the other hand, after a thorough review of the evidence, another study concluded that

> there is little reliable empirical evidence to support the existence of more than token—5 percent—disguised unemployment in underdeveloped countries as defined by zero marginal product of labor and the condition of *ceteris paribus*. [Kao et al., 1964, p. 141]

Schultz [1964], who was one of the principal authors of the 1951 study, had reversed himself by 1964, and argued that there was little or no disguised unemployment in rural areas in that the marginal productivity of labor was positive and therefore labor could not be withdrawn from rural areas without reducing output. Hansen [1969, 1971] came to a similar conclusion in an analysis of a study of employment and wages in rural Egypt, although there was rather substantial surplus labor during the slack season.

However, the academic arguments that characterized the discussions of rural unemployment during the 1950s and 1960s now seem sterile. Levels of income and consumption, not labor utilization per se, are the main determinants of living conditions, and for large numbers of rural people, incomes and consumption have apparently been stagnant or even deteriorating. And although most rural workers probably do contribute something to production, many of them produce very little. Underutilization of labor, meaning low levels of productivity, income, and consumption, may be as prevalent in rural as in urban areas.

Causes of Rural Unemployment

Unemployment is the result of labor supply exceeding labor demand at the prevailing returns to work. The higher the unemployment rate, the greater the labor surplus. The labor force is growing rapidly because those cohorts that are now entering the working ages are the product of the high population growth rates of the last two decades. Many factors modify the size and growth of the labor force, among the most important being the proportion of the potential labor force in school and attitudes toward female employment. However, labor-force growth during the next fifteen years is basically already determined; these individuals are already born. A decline in population growth rates in the near future would slow the labor-force growth rate in the more distant future, but there is little that can be done to slow labor force growth during the next two decades. Consequently, solutions to unemployment must focus on stimulating demand for and better utilization of labor.

Inadequate labor utilization in rural areas is largely the consequence of an inappropriate set of development policies and practices, particularly the following, many of which also contribute to slow growth in urban wage employment [see Eicher et al., 1970]:

1. Utilization of production techniques that are inappropriate to the existing resource endowment. This is to a large extent the consequence of growth strategies that view economic development solely or primarily as a function of savings and capital formation as modeled after Western experience. Many new technologies used in the agricultural sectors of low-income countries were developed in the West and suited for Western conditions of abundant skilled labor and capital. They are inconsistent with the conditions of scarce capital and abundant unskilled labor in low-income countries. Their use results in overutilization of scarce capital and underutilization of abundant labor.

2. This bias is aggravated by continued research and development—nearly all of which is conducted in the high-income world—producing capital-using and labor-displacing innovations. Singer [1970, p. 13] estimates that only 1 percent of the world's expenditure on scientific and technical research takes place in the low-income world. Large farm machinery companies and chemical and other agricultural industries—mostly in North America and Europe—as well as publicly supported research in these same countries account for most of the world's advances in agricultural technology.

3. Government policies compound these distortions in resource use by underpricing capital through artificially low interest rates, subsidies, overvalued exchange rates, preferential licensing of capital equipment imports, investment credits, depreciation allowances, and tariff rebates. As a result, agricultural mechanization usually is subsidized. For example, calculated in terms of wheat, a tractor costs twice as much in Iowa as in Pakistan; in Ivory Coast a loan for farm equipment can be financed at one-half what it costs in Germany [de Vries, 1972, p. 12]. According to Ridker [1971, p. 45], correcting such factor price distortions increased both employment and the rate of economic growth in Taiwan and South

Korea and to a lesser extent in (West) Pakistan, Indonesia, and historical Japan.

4. Production *disincentives* frequently further discourage expansion of labor-using sectors. Taxes often are levied on exports of primary products whose production is typically labor intensive. Marketing boards that artificially depress farm prices through their monopolistic buying are still in many countries a principal source of public revenue [Helleiner, 1970].

5. Wage labor is typically institutionally overvalued (thereby depressing employment growth) because of minimum wage and other social legislation and trade union pressures. Even in the agricultural sector, employment in plantation or other forms of estate agriculture sometimes is held down by legislation or practices that overpay labor without provisions to insure maximum employment and to limit labor-displacing mechanization.

6. Institutional structures—especially land tenure arrangements—limit the productive resources available to a substantial proportion of the rural population largely to their own labor; they have little or no land or other capital to augment their labor and to increase the return of their work efforts. In many countries this is aggravated further by the political power of the advantaged, which allows entrenchment of policies disadvantageous to the poor and powerless.

7. Real productivity is usually higher in urban industrial employment than in the rural employment alternatives. This is intensified by the tendency for urban industrial labor productivity to increase rapidly, often more or less offsetting the employment-generating effects of industrial growth. A variety of factors contribute to labor productivity gains, including (a) rising capital-labor ratios (due to capital-intensive expansion), (b) scale economies, (c) fuller utilization of existing capabilities of employed labor, (d) on-the-job training, and (e) increased labor efficiency arising from experience.

8. Rural public works programs have generally not generated employment commensurate with their potential. John P. Lewis [1971, pp. 18–20] believes this is because such programs have suffered from (a) small-scale thinking, (b) poor and hasty planning produced by an emergency mentality, (c) bureaucratic unwillingness to decentralize organization and control, (d) bad maintenance of completed projects, and (e) failure to coordinate the projects with the overall spatial development strategy. Despite this catalogue of disappointments, Lewis [pp. 29–30] not only makes a strong case for massive new initiatives in public works programs as a means of generating large-scale rural employment and attaining more equal distributions of income, he also argues that one of the major bottlenecks to such programs in the past—namely, highly inadequate and inelastic food supplies—has now been overcome by the green revolution breakthroughs.

The countries with the greatest public-works opportunities are those now achieving agricultural accelerations. On the one hand, the latter promise higher yields for a variety of rural works projects. On the other hand they are relaxing the food-supply constraints on incremental labor-intensive investment. [Lewis, 1971, p. 45]

In addition to their desirable impact on employment and income distribution, rural public works programs can (a) slow migration out of rural areas, (b) provide rural sectors with essential infrastructure such as roads, electricity, and water-control structures, and (c) expand effective demand in rural areas for both food and nonfood domestically produced labor-intensive goods.

9. Finally, a host of development strategies and policies overallocate resources to urban areas and underallocate resources to the rural sector, further contributing to the prevailing urban bias. In addition to high wages paid to government workers and others protected by strong urban trade unions, these include better public services such as education, sanitation, health services, transportation, and entertainment. Other public policies such as government pricing, taxation, and subsidies turn the terms of trade in favor of cities and against rural activities, further distorting rural-urban incomes and living conditions. All these practices reinforce the inherent prestige of urban life, which may in part be a legacy of the colonial period and a consequence of urban life styles of colonial administrators and the local elites who have replaced them. The net effect is to further increase the urban-rural income differential, further stimulate rural-to-urban migration, and hold down urban employment growth. Harris and Todaro have developed a model in which migration is a function of the expected rural-urban income differential [Todaro, 1969; Harris and Todaro, 1970; Todaro, 1971]. They show that an urban "unemployment equilibrium" will exist as long as urban wage rates are higher than the levels that would be dictated by market forces. If the income from urban jobs is sufficiently higher than rural incomes, migrants will be attracted to urban areas even if the probability of finding a job is low. Policies that attempt to reduce urban unemployment by creating more urban jobs without altering the prevailing structural inequalities in incomes and services will fail because, as more jobs are created and the probability of acquiring a job rises, more migrants will be attracted from rural areas. Todaro [1969, p. 140] cites as evidence the rise in the number of urban migrants in Kenya following the attempt by the government to create 15 percent more urban jobs through the Tripartite Agreement of 1964, which required employers to hire more workers. Although the Harris-Todaro model has some theoretical limitations and has not yet undergone adequate empirical testing [Byerlee, 1971, pp. 12–13], it nevertheless provides strong support for the proposition that urban unemployment rates can be brought down only by reducing the urban-

rural income differential and thereby reducing the relative attractiveness of urban life.

Income Distribution

If a single development goal were to be specified it would probably not be "full employment" but, rather, "adequate incomes." Although data on income distribution are scarce and frequently unreliable and there are no time series data at all for most low-income countries, available evidence generally shows two trends over the past two decades: (1) overall income distributions within low-income countries have become *more* skewed, and (2) rural per capita incomes have declined relative to urban per capita incomes.

Simon Kuznets [1955, 1966, 1971], who pioneered the study of the income distribution effects of economic development, concluded that inequality generally tends to widen in the earlier stages of economic development and later narrows, eventually resulting in greater equality than in the premodern period. Thus, the observed trends in income distribution in low-income countries are consistent with what the historical record might lead us to expect. But some economists and other development specialists are becoming alarmed about the unlikely prospects of a self-generating, more egalitarian future.

In this section it is argued that the structure of income distribution in low-income countries is highly unequal, and for most of the population, incomes are far from "adequate." Second, at least in some countries inequalities are increasing. Third, a highly unequal distribution of income is not only inherently inconsistent with development, but it is an obstacle to economic growth primarily by holding down domestic aggregate demand and distorting demand away from domestically produced labor-intensive commodities. It is further argued that such inequality delays within families the modernization process that is a prerequisite to spontaneous fertility decline and thus sets back the positive contribution to growth and development—at both the family and the macro levels—which would be the consequence of fertility decline.[3]

---

[3] The term "equality" rather than "equity" has been used even though the former is sometimes awkward semantically (for example, strictly speaking, incomes cannot become "more equal" since "equal" implies an absolute from which there can be no deviations, although in common usage the terms "more" and "less" are used to denote comparative degrees of equality and that practice will be followed here). "Equity," however, implies a moral or ethical value judgment concerning what is "just" or "right." While many people believe that if an income distribution became less skewed the result would also be more equitable, some people in higher income brackets whose incomes declined might feel the equity had decreased. The word "equality" has less potential for ambiguity in this respect.

Patterns and Trends in Income Distribution

Data on income distribution are notoriously difficult to collect and often of questionable reliability.[4] Further problems arise in intercountry comparisons because the original data are almost invariably collected and usually analyzed by different researchers with their own particular assumptions, techniques, and biases. In general, the larger the number of countries being compared, the more caution should be exercised in interpreting the results. This study will rely on the work of Oshima [1970], who studied in great detail most of the available data on income distributions in South and East Asia, and Cline [1971], who recently analyzed data on income distribution in four Latin American countries.[5] Income distribution schedules divided into decile shares are presented in Table 3.2 for the seven Asian countries studied by Oshima and two of the four Latin American countries studied by Cline.[6]

Although considerable caution should be exercised when comparing data compiled by two different researchers for two different cultural regions, these data are sufficiently interesting and (hopefully) accurate to warrant the comparisons made in Table 3.3, where the countries listed in Table 3.2 are grouped according to more and less equal income distributions. In each of the five countries in the less equal group, the poorest 30 percent of the population has less than 9 percent of the income, while the top half of the population has at least 80 percent of the income, and the top 10 percent has over 36 percent of the total income.

---

[4] For a discussion of some problems of measurement and analysis, see Turnham, 1971b.

[5] Another study analyzing selected economic, social, and political correlates of income distribution in forty-four primarily low-income countries is that of Adelman and Morris (1971a, 1971b). Among their forty-four countries, they have income distribution data on six of the nine countries in Table 3.2. Their data are identical to those of Oshima and Cline for Sri Lanka and Mexico and nearly identical for the Philippines. However, the Adelman-Morris data show slightly less income concentration for Brazil and considerably more concentration for Japan and Taiwan. Nevertheless, the ranking of these six countries by income concentration using their data is identical to that of Table 3.3. The works of Oshima and Cline have been utilized rather than that of Adelman and Morris primarily because (1) it would not be possible to discuss the demographic and rural development aspects as related to income distributions of most of the countries covered by Adelman and Morris primarily because of inadequate data but also lack of time and space. Fortunately, the same is not true for the countries analyzed by Cline and Oshima; (2) Adelman and Morris relied entirely on secondary sources for data on all forty-four countries, and the variability in data quality, concepts, and so forth, is probably substantially greater among their forty-four countries than among the smaller number studied in greater depth by Oshima and Cline; and (3) Adelman and Morris grouped their distributions only into quintiles instead of deciles, and did not include three countries that are analyzed here—South Korea, Malaya (West Malaysia), and Thailand.

[6] Argentina and Venezuela were studied by Cline but omitted from Table 3.2, primarily because they are not discussed in the later analysis of rural development and fertility decline. As for their income distributions, both fall in the middle range among the other nine countries—less skewed than Brazil and Mexico but more skewed than South Korea, Japan, and Taiwan (see Table 3.3).

Of the four countries with relatively equal income distribution, per capita income in Taiwan in 1961 (see Table 3.2) was only about one-third the level of Japan and West Malaysia (formerly Malaya) and about equal to that of South Korea.[7] Of course both Japan and Taiwan, and to a lesser extent South Korea, experienced remarkable growth in GNP during the 1960s. At the other extreme, Brazil—with a per capita income more than double that of Taiwan in 1961—had the most unequal income distribution of the nine countries. Mexico, with a per capita income a little larger than Brazil's in 1961 and about double that of Brazil in 1969, had a slightly less unequal income distribution. Thailand and Sri Lanka had per capita incomes similar to that of South Korea, and the Philippines had a per capita income considerably higher in 1961, but all three had substantially less equal income distributions than that of South Korea.

There are many problems in comparing rural and urban incomes, not the least of which is assigning a value to nonmonetized food and other home-produced goods [see Turnham, 1971b]. But when these adjustments have been made, available data suggest that average rural incomes and levels of living are almost universally lower than average urban incomes and levels of living. For example, in 1970 income per worker in Brazil averaged US$697 annually, but income per worker in the nonagricultural sector averaged $992, while income in agriculture averaged only $282 [Fishlow, 1972, p. 339]. Moreover, there is evidence that at least in some countries the distribution of incomes and wealth is no more equal—and in some cases is even less equal —in rural areas than overall. In Mexico, incomes are considerably less equally distributed within the rural sector than within the urban sector, despite the fact that the average rural family income is only *half* the average urban family income [Weisskoff, 1970, pp. 33–34]. The top 5 percent of rural income recipients earn as much as the top 5 percent of urban income recipients. In many countries the rural landed class is politically dominant and consequently enjoys only modest tax rates. According to Lele and Mellor [1972, p. 26], in India "upper-income rural people pay only about one-third as much in taxes as urban people in the same income bracket." Oshima found that in those Asian countries with greater income inequality— Thailand, the Philippines, and Sri Lanka—the rural-urban income character-istics were a major cause of the greater inequality. First, the rural income distribution is itself more unequal than the urban distribution. Second, the

---

[7] Malaysia is made up of the former Federation of Malaya (now called West Malaysia) and the states of Sarawak and Sabah (together comprising East Malaysia). Of a total population of 10 million at the end of 1968, 8.5 million were in West Malaysia (Malaya) [Marzuki and Peng, 1970, p. 1]. The 1961 estimate of per capita GNP for Malaya—US$368—is inexplicably high. Estimated gross domestic product per capita for 1958 was $217 and for 1963, $254 [GDP estimates from United Nations, 1965b, pp. 493–497; population estimates from U.N. *Monthly Bulletin of Statistics*, various numbers]. The latter figures are more in line with estimated per capita GNP in 1969 of $340.

TABLE 3.2   Comparison of size distribution of family income, selected countries, by income share of decile group

Country	Per capita income 1961	Per capita income 1969	Year	Share (in percent) of total income for each decile group D_1	D_2	D_3	D_4	D_5	D_6	D_7	D_8	D_9	D_{10}	Total
Brazil	$268	$270	1960	1.4	1.6	2.3	3.3	4.1	5.1	6.2	6.5	11.6	58.0	100.1
Mexico	297	580	1963	1.7	2.0	3.4	3.4	5.2	6.1	7.8	12.4	16.4	41.6	100.0
Japan	383	1,430	1963	3.0	4.7	5.7	7.3	7.9	9.0	10.4	12.0	16.0	24.0	100.0
Taiwan	116	300	1964	3.0	4.8	5.7	6.9	7.6	8.9	9.8	13.2	13.8	26.3	100.0
South Korea	106	210	1966	4.0	5.0	7.0	7.0	9.0	9.0	11.0	12.0	15.0	21.0	100.0
Philippines	188	210	1965	1.1	2.9	3.0	4.7	5.8	6.9	9.0	11.6	15.0	40.0	100.0
Thailand	101	160	1962	2.8	2.9	3.1	4.1	5.1	6.8	8.2	9.3	14.7	43.0	100.0
West Malaysia	368	340	1958	2.6	3.9	6.1	5.1	7.2	8.5	10.3	12.4	16.1	27.8	100.0
Sri Lanka	123	190	1963	1.5	3.0	4.0	5.2	6.3	7.5	9.0	11.2	15.5	36.8	100.0

SOURCES: Cline, 1971, Table I, p. 17; Oshima, 1970, Table 1, p. 13; per capita income estimates for 1961 (in 1961 dollars) are from Rosenstein-Rodan, 1961, Tables 1-A and 2-C, pp. 118 and 126; per capita income estimates for 1969 (in 1969 dollars) are from World Bank, 1971.

TABLE 3.3 Comparison of size distribution and relative equality of family income for selected countries, by more and less equal distribution groups

Country	Lower deciles $D_1 + D_2 + D_3$		Middle deciles $D_4 + D_5 + D_6 + D_7$		Upper deciles $D_8 + D_9 + D_{10}$		Top decile	Sum of decile deviations from 10 percent	Ratio: top 2 deciles to bottom 2 deciles
			GROUP A: MORE EQUAL DISTRIBUTIONS						
South Korea	16.0	(5.3)	36.6	(9.0)	38.0	(12.7)	21.0	38	4.0 : 1
Japan	13.4	(4.5)	34.6	(8.7)	52.0	(17.3)	24.0	45	5.2 : 1
Taiwan	13.5	(4.5)	33.2	(8.3)	53.3	(17.8)	26.3	47	5.1 : 1
West Malaysia	12.6	(4.2)	33.1	(7.8)	56.3	(18.8)	27.8	52	6.8 : 1
			GROUP B: LESS EQUAL DISTRIBUTIONS						
Sri Lanka	8.5	(2.8)	28.0	(7.0)	63.5	(21.2)	36.8	67	11.6 : 1
Philippines	7.0	(2.3)	26.4	(6.6)	66.6	(22.2)	40.0	74	13.8 : 1
Thailand	8.8	(2.9)	24.2	(6.1)	67.0	(22.3)	43.0	76	10.1 : 1
Mexico	7.1	(2.4)	22.5	(5.6)	70.4	(23.5)	41.6	82	15.7 : 1
Brazil	5.3	(1.8)	18.7	(4.7)	76.1	(25.4)	58.0	99	23.2 : 1

SOURCE: Adapted from Table 3.2.

NOTE: Figures in parentheses are average shares per decile.

rural mean and median incomes are much lower in absolute size than the urban mean and median incomes.

Size of landholdings is a good indicator of the distribution of wealth and levels of living in rural India. At the poorest end, 42 percent cultivate either no land at all or less than one acre; altogether they cultivate 1.3 percent of the total cultivated land [Abel, 1971, p. 29]. This means that on the average, each of the bottom four deciles has about 0.4 percent of the total cultivated land. At the other extreme, 12 percent of the households cultivate holdings of ten acres or more, accounting for 59 percent of total cultivated land.

An analysis of the agricultural income distribution in Colombia in 1960 indicates that the top decile received over 52 percent of total agricultural income. The bottom 50 percent received 16 percent of the total income. There is evidence that the distribution of rural incomes became more skewed during the period 1930–1960 [Berry, 1972, pp. 404–405].

Available data suggest that at least in some countries income distributions have become more skewed in recent years. One study found this trend from 1950 to the early 1960s in Puerto Rico, Argentina, Mexico, and Colombia [Weisskoff, 1970]. A careful analysis of the income distribution in Brazil found that

> the conclusion that inequality has increased over the course of the decade seems correct, if lamentable. The upper 3.2 percent of the labor force commands 33.1 percent of the income in 1970, compared to about 27 percent in 1960. [Fishlow, 1972, p. 399]

In Kenya from 1960 to 1966, average urban wages rose twice as fast as average agricultural incomes; in 1966, agricultural incomes were less than one-half the level of incomes of unskilled urban wage earners [Ghai, 1968, p. 20]. The rural-urban income differential in Nigeria has widened consistently since 1955; in 1965 average farm earnings were only one-third the urban unskilled wage rate [Byerlee, 1972, p. 65]. In Zambia from 1956 to 1968 the government minimum wage increased about threefold and average earnings of African urban workers increased about 3.5 times, while rural income per household increased only 14 percent [Knight, 1971]. From 1954 to 1964 in Uganda, the share of income going to rural peasants declined, while the share going to wage earners in the modern sector increased. In 1964 the average earnings of wage employees was about three times the value of output per worker on the land [Knight, 1968, 1971]. Knight cautions that little reliance should be placed on the precise magnitudes of these changes, but he feels that the data probably do reflect the relative changes in rural and urban income inequality.[8]

---

[8] In comparing rural and urban incomes and their absolute and relative changes over time, among the more serious difficulties are determining what is the most appropriate definition(s) of income, how to take account of nonmonetized production and consumption, differential costs of living and access to social services, and sharing of incomes [Knight, 1971; Byerlee and Eicher, 1972, pp. 25–28].

From 1960–1971 to 1967–1968, the number of the "poor" in rural India increased from about 144 million to between 165 and 206 million. "Poor" was defined as an income less than 15 rupees per person monthly, which was considered too low to provide a bare minimum level of subsistence [Abel, 1971, pp. 23–26].

> While there appeared to be a trend toward reduction in inequities of rural incomes during the 1950s, analysis for the 1960s would suggest that, at best, the distribution of incomes remained the same. However, there is some evidence to suggest that inequalities actually increased. [Abel, 1971, p. 26]

In summary, while it may not be valid to generalize from these few cases to most of the low-income world, the accumulating evidence clearly shows that at least for some important countries, which together contain a substantial proportion of the population of the low-income world, income distributions have not improved in recent years and in some cases they have apparently become more skewed. Moreover, average rural incomes seem universally lower than average urban incomes, and in some countries incomes are apparently even more skewed in rural than in urban areas.

Income Distribution, Savings, and Economic Growth

One cannot discuss income distribution and development without discussing savings. During the 1950s and 1960s the conventional wisdom of economic development assumed that the "capitalist" or "modern" sector had a much higher propensity to save than the "labor" or "traditional" sector. Since the process of development was at the same time generally seen as capital accumulation to maximize the rate of growth of national income,[9] the logical policy prescription for the short run at least was "put income into the hands of the savers"—that is, the capitalist class.[10] As a matter of fact, the logical extension of this reasoning is that the more unequal the income distribution, the higher the savings rate and the more rapid the rate of economic growth. Thus, a skewed income distribution that over a period of time is becoming even more skewed is highly desirable! Lele and Mellor have called these savings-maximizing development theories the "bourgeois approach."

> It was also believed that minimizing employment and thereby consumption in the short run would conserve resources so that they could be ploughed back into further expansion of the manufacturing sector. The conclusions that follow from such assumptions may be stated succinctly but simplistically

---

[9] The Harrod-Domar model of development, popular during this period, postulates economic growth as a constant function of savings (investment).

[10] In the Lewis model, savings as a proportion of national income is assumed to increase as the "modern" or "profit-making" sector becomes larger relative to the traditional sector.

as follows: the lower the rate of growth of employment and consumption in the short run, the higher their levels in the long run. It is a bourgeois approach, for it is the poor who die in the short run. [Lele and Mellor, 1972, p. 23]

In recent years these assumptions about economic behavior have been assailed from many sides. First, concepts of "physical capital" and its accumulation have generally been too narrowly defined. For example, in densely populated rural areas a great deal of nonconventional "capital formation" frequently takes place, especially in slack seasons, in the form of repairing irrigation channels, land leveling, drainage works, and so forth.

Second, evidence does *not* show that in the low-income world lower income recipients are necessarily poor savers while only higher income recipients are good savers. In fact, in many low-income countries—and particularly in Latin American countries over a long period up to the present—recipients of large incomes have often demonstrated a high propensity to consume imported luxury goods and to "salt away" investment funds in foreign countries rather than to make domestic employment-generating investments. Seers stresses the potential for domestic surplus to be frittered away by the high import propensities of the wealthy.

A high import coefficient is to be expected in a country where the incomes and consumer habits reflect those of far richer countries . . . naïve growth theory normally stresses the tendency of savings propensities to be higher among higher income groups and ignores the effect on import propensities; it therefore implies that inequality is unequivocally helpful to development. [Seers, 1969, pp. 227–228]

Oshima [1970, p. 32] found that in Asia high personal savings are associated with *more*, not less, equal income distributions.

Third, in low-income countries the public rather than the private sector is commonly the major source of domestic savings (savings defined conventionally and narrowly). In general, it is not clear in what manner the incidence of public savings is distributed over the various categories of income recipients. But income and property taxes are notoriously difficult to administer and collect in low-income countries, and in a number of countries marketing boards and export taxes in primary products still account for a large share of domestic public savings, and frequently this falls disproportionately on lower income recipients. Thus, while income tax structures in low-income countries are usually progressive, other taxes are generally regressive, so that on balance high-income recipients may not pay a much larger proportion of their incomes in taxes than do low-income recipients. Few data are available, but in Colombia in 1966 the incidence of all taxes averaged 14 percent, but the range was narrow—from a low of about 12 percent for the lowest income brackets to only about 17 percent for the highest income brackets [ILO, 1970, p. 144].

Fourth, "capital formation" has generally not been defined to include "human" capital, but there is growing evidence that human capital formation may well be a more important determinant of economic growth and development than is physical capital. The well-known Denison studies of the determinants of growth in Europe and North America found that accumulation of physical capital played a relatively minor role. On the other hand, during the first half of this century in the United States, "education" and "advance in knowledge" (roughly, technological advance) together were apparently responsible for nearly one-half of total growth [Denison, 1962]. Labor-force growth contributed another one-quarter, and physical capital contributed considerably less.

Finally and most significantly, for many low-income countries lack of effective *demand* for domestically produced labor-intensive products may be a more severe constraint on economic growth than is inadequate savings. Cline's study of the effects of a hypothetical income redistribution on economic growth in four Latin American countries concluded that

> on balance, the very large weight of agriculture and foodstuffs in the increased demand suggests that income redistribution would raise overall economic efficiency by shifting demand to a sector with low factor opportunity cost (land and labor) and away from sectors with high factor opportunity cost (capital). . . . The major policy implication is that even under conservative assumptions income redistribution would not do irreparable damage to economic growth, and the growth costs could be regarded as very reasonable in comparison with the resulting equity gains. [Cline, 1971, pp. 22–23]

Regarding the agricultural sector in particular, Eicher [1969] argues that the importance of effective demand has been underestimated, resulting in a "supply approach" to development. Policies that improve the incomes of small farmers would stimulate economic growth by increasing the effective demand for domestically produced agricultural and nonagricultural products. Oshima graphically describes how, during the process of economic growth and modernization, labor-intensive sectors—both agricultural and nonagricultural—interact with each other in purchasing products and supplying inputs, thereby augmenting effective demand for each other's products. He suggests conceptualizing the economies of most Asian countries as overlapping three-ring circuses, where the first ring is the agricultural sector, the second is the nonfarm labor-intensive sector, and the third is the commercial sector.

> In the second labor-intensive sector, proprietors and their family help and employees work for each other and buy each other's products, whether in manufacturing, transport, services, construction, or trade. This sector overlaps considerably with the agricultural sector, buying food, raw materials, and other inputs and employing off-season farm workers while selling manufactured food, clothing, housing, implements, etc. . . . Consequently, when

there is an increase in demand, from, say, the agricultural sector, much of this is transmitted to the labor-intensive sector in nonagriculture. In two countries where, beginning with land reform, agricultural output and productivity have been growing most rapidly, Japan and Taiwan, unemployment is lowest and the small industries appear to be operating at full capacity. This is to be expected not only from the demand side (that is, the increase in the purchasing power of farmers for traditional and wage goods) but also from the input side, for much of the raw materials of small industries (for food, clothing, and housing implements) is of local origin. [Oshima, 1971, p. 170]

Johnston [1966, p. 275] shows that during the process of Japanese development three sectors, which he calls agriculture, "semimodern" nonagriculture, and "modern" nonagriculture, interacted with each other in a manner similar to that described by Oshima above. Byerlee and Eicher [1972] suggest that in Africa there are in reality four sectors, three of which would usually be labor intensive: (1) the agricultural production sector, (2) the rural small-scale nonagricultural sector, (3) the urban small-scale nonagricultural sector, and (4) the urban large-scale nonagriculture sector. Whatever the most appropriate disaggregation, these analyses all emphasize the stimulus to growth that intersector demand can generate.

Preoccupation with savings and physical capital accumulation led to the development philosophy of growth *first*, equality later. Basic to this view is the assumption that once the appropriate economic structure is in place and the economy has reached the stage of self-sustaining growth, mechanisms will be available that will permit a more equal sharing of the fruits of growth. This is all quite consistent with Kuznets' findings that Western economies first experienced a worsening and only later an improvement in income distribution. Unfortunately this process shows little promise of repeating itself in contemporary low-income countries. The Yale Economic Growth Center found that

> there seems to be little evidence in favor of the "trickle down" theory of economic development, according to which if only adequate output growth can be successfully achieved, distribution or, more precisely, the welfare of the people on the bottom end of the distribution, will take care of itself via demand interactions in the system . . . distribution is likely to worsen, especially if a "capital-intensive" path of development is chosen . . . there is little evidence that this form of development is self-correcting in the sense that market forces will ultimately tend to pull the system out of this path. [Yale Economic Growth Center, 1971, pp. 5–6]

Causes of Income Inequality

It has been argued that the primary causes of prevailing and, in some cases, worsening income inequalities are development policies and institutional structures that favor the owners of capital and land at the expense of laborers. In the first category are those policies that subsidize the use of capital, thereby increasing the share of income going to capital and decreasing the share going to labor. These were itemized in the earlier section on causes of rural underemployment. The pattern of technological change appears to be a particularly important cause of this type of distorted development. Berry [1970] has constructed alternate economic models of developing countries and found that "neutral" technological change—change that saves both capital and labor in equal proportions—would in the short run generally worsen income distribution but in the long run improve it. But because low-income countries are "borrowing" from high-income countries technology that is suited to labor-scarce endowments, Berry finds that technological change in low-income countries is almost invariably labor saving, and that countries are introducing this labor-saving technology at a far earlier stage of their development process than did the high-income countries. As long as technology continues to be borrowed, the "automatic corrective" devices of technology responding to factor endowments and consequently *improving* income distribution will not function. As a result, Berry expects a more negative trend in income distribution over time than that which occurred in the high-income countries. Since income distributions are already highly skewed, he is quite pessimistic about future income distribution prospects [Berry, 1970, pp. 34–36].

In the second category are agrarian institutions, which serve as disincentives to labor utilization and limit the share of output going to labor. Thiesenhusen [1971b] argues that with the prevailing distribution of land ownership in most of Latin America, the consequence of technological change and output expansion in agriculture will be an even more unequal income distribution. Whatever the prospects for a green revolution in Latin America, Thiesenhusen sees no hope of an improved distribution of rural incomes without thoroughgoing agrarian reform. Even more seriously, these policies and institutions create an economic, social, and political structure that is not only self-perpetuating but self-strengthens as time goes on, making the initial situation even worse.

According to Oshima, the main reasons that income distributions in Southeast Asian countries are more unequal than in East Asian countries are as follows:

> Yields per acre of rice and other crops are substantially lower in the Southeast Asian countries, from one-third to one-half those of East Asian countries. Moreover, due to the lack of irrigation and other inputs, the extent of double-cropping is limited compared with the extensive double-cropping in East Asia (despite the colder climate), making for structural underemployment in the former of about one-third to one-fourth per year. Sharecropping and other forms of tenancy, largely in the more fertile rice valleys and plains of Southeast Asia close to the large cities, are extensive compared to the

situation in East Asia where drastic land reform was carried out in the immediate postwar years. About half of the rice crops of between one-half and two-thirds of farm families in the rice valleys and plains of Thailand and Philippines are turned over to landlords, many of whom live in the metropolis and other cities, augmenting the incomes of the upper deciles in the urban areas. As to estate or plantation agriculture (which is labour-intensive), incomes paid to workers are by no means high, from extremely low in the sugar plantations of the Visayas in the Philippines to moderately low in the tea and rubber plantations of Ceylon [Sri Lanka] and Thailand. The owners of the plantations also live in the cities. There are no plantations in East Asia. [Oshima, 1970, p. 25]

There is little disagreement—except from the Marxists—that rapid population growth itself is an important cause of worsening income distributions in the low-income world. As discussed above, the sources of income for poorer people are largely limited to their relatively unskilled labor. Thus, growth in their incomes depends primarily on growth in wages or agricultural earnings. By contrast, higher income recipients have additional income-producing sources, particularly their more skilled labor and, for many, the ownership of property. Even unskilled industrial workers usually belong to trade unions, which provide additional earning power. Thus, even if population growth rates were *similar* for both low- and high-income groups, per capita income would normally be increasing more rapidly for the higher income groups because of their greater income-earning opportunities, further skewing an already highly skewed income distribution.

The fact that both fertility and population growth rates are almost always higher among low-income groups further skews the overall income distribution. Daly argues that the capitalist (high-income) class has control over both the means of (economic) production as well as reproduction (fertility), while the poorer class controls neither.

A capitalist monopoly on the means of production becomes coupled with a simultaneous monopoly on the means of limiting reproduction. By withholding contraception from the working class, while at the same time limiting its own numbers, the capitalist class shares the exploited surplus among fewer people. The personal distribution of income becomes even more concentrated. [Daly, 1971, p. 31]

According to Daly [1970, pp. 569–570], high- and low-income classes obey different "laws" of population: "The lower class is limited by its aggregate wealth, the upper class by its standard of living." He shows that if aggregate income is growing at 6.5 percent annually for both high- and low-income classes, but if high-income families average four children while low-income families average eight children, then lower class per capita income will increase by a factor of 1.2 (20 percent) each generation while upper class per capita income will increase by a factor of 2.4 (140 percent) each generation. Applying the analysis to northeastern Brazil, he concludes that,

> allowing for the strong likelihood that lower-class total income grows at less than, and upper-class income at more than, the assumed 6.5 percent annually, we may consider lower-class per capita income as constant (or possibly decreasing), and upper-class per capita income as increasing by more than 2.4 times per generation. [Daly, 1970, p. 571]

Using Mauritius as a case in point, Meade argues that in a society characterized by a very unequal distribution of ownership of property, efforts to improve the living conditions of the poorest class, who have only their unskilled labor as a source of income, will fail as a result of either very low wages or very high rates of unemployment. If the wage rate is maintained high enough to secure a decent living for wage earners, then there will be high unemployment. If the wage rate is low enough to result in full employment, workers' incomes will be very low.

> Thus *either* there is unemployment or underemployment of labor, since there is not enough land and capital to equip all available workers in current lines of production, *or else* the wage-rate must fall very low indeed to encourage the introduction of new lines of production, which employ much labor with little equipment of capital or land and which become profitable only when labor is very cheap relatively to land and capital. [Meade, 1967, p. 237][11]

Rapid population growth of the laboring class increases the supply of labor relative to land and capital, intensifies the low income-high unemployment dilemma, and worsens the prevailing highly unequal distribution of incomes between property owners and wage earners. Meade sees no solution to this dilemma short of drastic redistribution of property rights and wealth or drastic population control.

In an econometric model designed to test the relationships between population growth and income distribution, Lindert [1971] found that income inequality is seriously heightened by population growth. His model yields a vicious circle of large-family poverty and small-family prosperity over the generations. This is because the distribution of *property* income is universally more unequal than the distribution of *wage* income. Population growth, by increasing the growth in the labor force, enlarges the number of workers among whom wage income must be divided and heightens the

---

[11] Meade [1967, p. 237] notes, however, that "in a community in which there was an equal distribution of the ownership of property these concomitant evils of overpopulation—namely, unemployment or unequal distribution of income—might not be serious," because "if each citizen were a representative property-owner as well as a representative worker, what he lost in wages he would gain in property income."

existing income inequality. The more rapid the growth in population and labor force, the greater the income maldistribution effect.[12]

In summary, this analysis suggests that rapid population growth further aggravates low incomes and poverty. But it also suggests that it is the prevailing social, political, and economic structure that is primarily responsible for perpetuating this vicious circle by preventing the poor from experiencing improved living conditions that would speed the modernization processes in their lives and motivate them to have smaller families. Moreover, most analysts appear pessimistic about the prospects for economic growth generating greater income equality—or even preventing greater inequality —in the near future. As for Brazil,

> in the absence of effective and far-reaching alteration in governmental attitudes, there is likely to be little progress and quite possibly, retrogression in the distribution of incomes. [Fishlow, 1972, p. 402]

One of the major conclusions from the Adelman-Morris study was that,

> in the absence of specific policy measures aimed at improving the distribution of income, there is, for the most part, a negative association between the rate of economic development and the share of income accruing to the poorest segment of the population. [Adelman and Morris, 1971b, Part I, p. 2]

Land Reform and Rural Development

Since in most countries the structure of the land-tenure system is probably the single most important determinant of the prevailing distribution of rural incomes and wealth as well as of future rural distributional prospects, the discussion of land tenure justifies a separate section. "Land reform" here

---

[12] In addition, economic-demographic models have consistently shown that lower rates of population growth in low-income countries would produce substantial economic benefits, including distributional benefits. Hoover [1971] and Robinson and Horlacher [1971] review much of this literature. For applications to India, see Coale and Hoover [1958] and Simmons [1971]. These models have some rather serious limitations and can generally be faulted for oversimplification, unsubstantiated assumptions, and inappropriate development goals—for example, the single objective of most is to maximize the rate of growth of per capita income. For critiques of these models see Myrdal [1968, pp. 2063–2075] and Leibenstein [1969]. Although for the most part little confidence should be placed in the precise magnitudes of the benefits of slower population growth given by these models, we can be reasonably confident that there would be benefits. Perhaps their most serious limitation is that they provide no useful policy prescriptions except to reduce poulation growth rates, but since the determinants of fertility behavior are generally not built into the models, they give no answers as to how to effectively reduce fertility. For lucid and nonmathematical discussions of this topic see Demeny [1971] and Schultz [1971, pp. 164–169].

means a redistribution of the rights of ownership and/or use of land away from large landowners and in favor of cultivators with little or no land-holdings. Measures that guarantee tenants greater security of cultivation rights and effectively limit the amount of rent that can be collected by the landowner—while not actually transferring ownership of the land—can sometimes achieve much the same objective, that is, higher incomes and greater economic security for farmers with low incomes. However, in the absence of an outright transfer of ownership, the gains to the beneficiaries of the land reform generally are more limited. The full benefits of land reform usually can be realized only if the redistribution of rights to land is accompanied by programs to provide adequate credit, essential purchased inputs, technical information, and market outlets for those farmers who have benefited from the reform. This more comprehensive set of changes usually is termed "agrarian reform."

In recent years the literature on agricultural development has been preoccupied with the green revolution developments and their production and distribution potentials. One consequence has been that less attention has been given to land reform. This does not indicate that land reform has become less urgent or that earlier proponents are now silent. Quite the contrary, many economists and other development specialists are now arguing that the emergence of the green revolution in Asia and its impending emergence in Latin America have created an even greater need for land reform. These advocates fear that existing inequalities of ownership will be aggravated as production breakthroughs make land more valuable, and that the existing distribution of rural political power and wealth will facilitate the further entrenchment of large landowners, making subsequent land redistribution more difficult and less likely and making the problems of income inequality less solvable. For Myrdal [1968, 1970], if there is a "key" to agricultural development in Asia, it is land reform.

Because much of rural Africa is sparsely populated with a fairly even distribution of landholdings (often communal) and primarily small-scale land-extensive forms of agriculture, there have been only limited pressures for land reform in Africa.[13] But in many Asian and Latin American countries it is perhaps the overriding social, economic, and political issue. A recent Food and Agricultural Organization [1971] report concluded that in many agricultural regions land reform remains a prerequisite for development. According to this report, the urgency for reform is greater now than ever before, primarily because (1) income inequalities and unemployment in rural areas have worsened, (2) rapid population growth promises to exacerbate existing inequalities, and (3) recent and potential technological

---

[13] Land reform has been carried out in areas of former white ownership in Kenya. Highly unequal landholdings are a barrier to better income distribution in rural areas of white-controlled southern Africa, and in parts of North Africa.

breakthroughs in agriculture will be exploited primarily by the rural advantaged and powerful and will result—as the consequence of prevailing agrarian structures—in the increase of their power, wealth, and capacity for resisting future reform. While land reform is essential, it is likely to be ineffective and perhaps counterproductive unless it changes rural institutions that control production and supporting services as well as land tenure. It must be accompanied by (1) the technical education of peasants, (2) improved agricultural extension methods, and (3) rural financial systems that serve peasants [FAO, 1971].

Unfortunately, in the 1960s less progress was made with agrarian reform than in each of the previous two decades [FAO, 1971]. Many countries passed land reform legislation, some of it very strict, but with few exceptions only token enforcement has resulted. In South Asia, for example,

> concerning the consequences of ownership ceiling and land redistribution measures . . . there have been no revolutionary disturbances in property relationships within the agrarian structure. Long-standing inequalities within the village structure have scarcely been touched. [Myrdal, 1968, p. 1320]

Proponents of land reform have always had to contend with the charge that a sacrifice in total output will be the inevitable consequence. The conventional interpretation of the Mexican land reforms of the 1920s and 1930s —that its "economic opportunity cost" was a decline in agricultural productivity—is partly responsible for this belief. This conclusion has given land reform a bad reputation and produced misleading generalizations about its economic impact. As Folke Dovring [1970] and others have recently documented, this misinterpretation of the Mexican experience was the product of bad data and deliberate government manipulation of statistics; the real impact of the Mexican land reform was increased productivity. While in the past three decades the private, large-scale farmers—especially in the less densely populated north and northwestern regions where there are few *ejidos* (communal holdings)—were able to greatly expand crop land, irrigation, mechanization, and agricultural output, the land reform areas had the disadvantages of poorer soil and greater population densities, with much less land and other resources per worker. However, through more intensive land use, many of these areas have been able to absorb excess manpower by cultivating higher value crops. This has resulted in higher yields and product values, which have kept pace with and in some cases surpassed those of the large-scale commercial sector. Dovring concludes that

> it is clear that the sociopolitical gains of the land reform have in no way been at the expense of economic progress. Land reform steered more of the nation's resources into labor intensive growth in agriculture, which is precisely what the country needed at the time and still needs for some time to come. [Dovring, 1970, p. 274]

Contrary to the prevailing belief, the Mexican experience is not atypical.

> The evidence available on post-reform experiences—in Mexico, Bolivia, Chile, Japan, Taiwan, Egypt—shows that although in some cases there was an initial drop, average productivity per unit of land increased rather substantially after these reforms. All cases involved a reduction in the average size of farm. [Dorner and Kanel, 1971, p. 54]

One of the reasons that yields usually rise following land reform is that cultivators who own the land they farm typically have both greater incentives and more resources for making land- and yield-improving investments since they receive all the benefits themselves. Myrdal [1968, p. 1068] cites a United Nations study that covered all regions of India and showed that in the early 1960s, landowners who cultivated their own land spent ten times as much on land improvements per hectare as landowners who leased out their land, and four times as much as tenants who did not own the land they cultivated. Many of these investments, such as construction and maintenance of irrigation works, are labor intensive. Farmers who own their own land can often do this work during the slack seasons when other labor requirements are low, thus increasing their overall labor productivity by partially offsetting the normal seasonal nature of farming.

Another reason that yields improve is that labor is used much more intensively, with more labor per land unit.

> While latifundios average 400 times larger than many tiny farms called minifundios, they employ only 15 times more workers. The reason for this phenomenon is not hard to find. Pressures for the adoption of labor-saving technology in Latin America are similar—if not yet so pervasive—as those in industry. Accordingly, the trend on large farms in Latin America is toward use of less and less labor per unit of output. [Thiesenhusen, 1971c, pp. 69–70]

The International Labour Organization [1970] strategy for employment generation in Colombia forcefully argued that the land tenure system is the critical constraint to greater labor absorption and growth in agricultural output. Based on his study of the determinants of income distribution in rural Colombia, Berry concluded that

> the data suggest strongly that *unless a solution is found largely outside the sector* there is no quick solution for the bad distribution of income in agriculture which does not involve land redistribution as an important component. [Berry, 1972, p. 408; italics in original]

For many countries in both Latin America and Asia, land reform is probably the most effective mechanism available for coping with the problem of productively utilizing a rapidly growing labor force in the years ahead and at the same time blunting or reversing the tendency toward greater income inequality.

Hayami and Ruttan recently reviewed the historic conditions under which land reform and technological change in agriculture combined to produce rapid gains in agricultural productivity. They concluded that circumstances are again ripe for agrarian reform to stimulate rapid growth in total agricultural output.

> Economic gains to be had from a radical modification in land tenure patterns will be greatest during periods when rapid technical changes are opening up new production possibilities which are inhibited by existing tenure relationships. . . . In our judgment, the current simultaneous incidence of a technical revolution in grain production and an explosive rate of growth in the agricultural labor force is again opening up the possibility of economic gains from modifications of land tenure relationships that are substantially greater than in the 1950s and 1960s in many developing countries. The embodiment of the new technical potentials in new crop varieties and in industrial inputs means that tenure systems which dampen incentives to use the new inputs will reduce both the production impact and the social returns from the new biological technology. And tenure systems which discourage the evolution of more labor-intensive systems of crop and livestock production will exacerbate the labor absorption problem. [Hayami and Ruttan, 1971, p. 263]

Oshima argues that a causal relationship has existed in Asia between land reform and growth and development. Japan and Taiwan carried out thorough land reform but the Philippines and Sri Lanka have not. For the latter two,

> their agricultural production has been sluggish, unemployment has been untractable, and the national growth rate is about one-half that of Japan and Taiwan. [Oshima, 1971, p. 174]

According to Dantwala, India now needs a "preventive land reform." By that he means measures that will effectively prevent big and advantaged farmers from acquiring more land and thus causing further disadvantages to smaller and weaker farmers. His reservations about stronger reform measures are that they would be difficult to implement and would probably result in less real benefit to small landowners and the landless than would more modest restrictions.

> Once some such innovation as a "miracle seed" shatters the technological barrier to rewarding human endeavor, economic and institutional policies acquire a grave responsibility of ensuring that the gains of technology are not monopolized by the privileged and the powerful. [Dantwala, 1970, p. 22]

A major study of the prospects for Nigerian agricultural development up to 1985 detailed the considerable development potential that was possible under the prevailing pattern of small-holder agriculture [Johnson et al., 1969]. Provided that adequate biological research were undertaken to develop improved varieties of staple foods, including nutritionally superior foods, the study showed that a pattern of small-holder agriculture would achieve the multiple goals of better labor utilization (more rural employment), improved incomes for small-scale agriculturalists, low food prices for urban-dwellers, and improved nutrition.

Not all economists agree that land reform and small-scale agriculture are consistent with both growth and development. In an analysis of Brazilian agricultural development prospects, Nicholls concluded that Brazil must choose either greater equality or higher productivity. After documenting the history of agricultural neglect, the highly dualistic agrarian structure that has resulted, and the severe maldistribution of resources and incomes within Brazilian agriculture (see Chapter 4), Nicholls comes out in favor of *production* rather than greater equality. He believes that only the already highly commercial sector has the resources and experience to generate future agricultural growth.

> Without concomitant financial and technical assistance, land reform is likely to be very ineffective; while, with adequate public service and continued industrial urban development, land reform can easily become a major impediment to agricultural modernization and general economic development. . . . for some time to come, Brazilian agriculture will probably continue to have an economy in which a modern large-scale sector and a primitive small-scale sector concurrently exist, often side by side. . . . [Agriculture] is likely to remain a sector of many rural people of low productivity and incomes whose *poverty* problem can be solved not by fixing them to the land but by making it possible for them to move out of agriculture into more productive and remunerative nonagricultural employment. [Nicholls, 1971, p. 388]

This conclusion is just the opposite of that of another study, which found that land reform in Brazil would *increase* the rate of growth of total agricultural output, primarily because smaller holdings cultivated by farmers who owned their own land would be used more intensively—as in Mexico—and as a result, yields would increase more rapidly [Cline, 1970]. Moreover, it is highly unlikely that Brazil will be able to generate urban employment sufficiently rapidly to absorb even the natural increase of the urban population let alone all those whose only alternative to urban migration is rural poverty. Brazilian unemployment statistics are notoriously bad, but it is generally believed that initial high rates of urban unemployment worsened during the 1960s [Jones, 1968, p. 463]. It has been estimated that Brazil must maintain an economic growth rate of 12 percent annually just to absorb the new entrants to the urban labor force, even without a policy of encouraging more rapid rural-to-urban migration [Thiesenhusen, 1971c, p. 61]. A deliberate policy of moving low-productivity rural people to the cities can only aggravate the urban unemployment problem and condemn more people to lifelong poverty.

Despite these contrary opinions, if "development" means more productive lives and improved living conditions, then it seems clear that in many countries thorough land reform can make a direct contribution to rural development. In some agricultural areas, existing agrarian structures effectively prevent development for the rural poor. In many countries of Latin America and Asia,

> if the agricultural sector is to make a greater contribution to overall development, basic reorganization and redistribution of land and capital are required in order to: productively employ more people in agriculture, contribute more to capital formation in both the agricultural and industrial sectors, and provide the income distribution necessary for broadening the market for locally manufactured goods as well as for the increased production from agriculture. [Dorner and Kanel, 1971, p. 55]

Land reform has the added benefit of reducing the relative attractiveness of urban life, and thereby may help dampen the rate of rural-to-urban migration and ease the burdens of urban unemployment and unrest. Finally, it will be argued in Chapter 4 that by improving the living conditions and stimulating the modernization process of rural people, land reform has the secondary effect of making a contribution to modernization and fertility decline.

Unfortunately, international assistance organizations have generally provided very few economic and technical resources in support of land reform. From 1950 to the end of 1968 the United States Agency for International Development (USAID) allocated more than US$200 million to support agricultural credit programs in Latin America and $70 million to support colonization programs but less than $30 million to programs that might be interpreted as promoting land reform. Likewise, the World Bank has done very little to promote land reform despite its substantial resources [Adams, 1970, p. 424]. According to Petras and LaPorte, during the 1960s the policy of USAID moved *away* from a redistributionist approach and toward a productionist approach to rural development. According to them, AID officials typically respond that

> everybody in the Agency [AID]—any economist—has argued himself out of it [a distributionist approach] for a number of reasons. First, land reform means a decrease in production. Second, it means a disruption of marketing and credit and transportation. Third, it's just too costly. Fourth, and it's not said overtly, land reform is against the tide of history. History shows that the trend has been the consolidation of land. . . . You can't resolve agricultural poverty. . . . Fifth, people are pessimistic about carrying the reform out. You just can't force vested interests to carry the load. [Petras and LaPorte, 1970, p. 263]

But Adams, while agreeing that the impetus for land reform must come from within the country, argues that

> aid agencies can, in many cases, make or break the effort. Lack of commitment by aid agencies to this issue may be almost as important in explaining the current state in land reform as landowners' resistance. [Adams, 1970, p. 432–433]

The major barrier to land reform, however, is usually the large landowners, who are almost always politically powerful and frequently politically, economically, and socially dominant; they stand to lose the most (at least in the short run) from land reform. They have generally been able to neutralize redistributionist sentiment and utilize economic change to augment their own power and wealth. The relatively few effective land reforms in recent decades are an indication of the strength and resistance of these groups. In some of the countries with more "successful" and thorough land reforms—for example, Japan, Taiwan, Mexico, Egypt—this obstacle has been overcome in conjunction with wars, revolutions, or authoritarian regimes. Yet this need not be a necessary precondition. In many countries meaningful reforms have been legislated; only implementation has been ineffective. In some of these countries—for example, India and Chile—popular support may have reached the point where effective land reforms will be implemented with little or no violence. It is argued in this paper that land reform together with the appropriate set of complementary institutional reforms will result in increased output, better utilization of labor, more equal distribution of incomes, and more rapid overall fertility decline. If governments in low-income countries together with international aid organizations can be persuaded that these will be the likely consequences of an effective land reform, the prospects for its successful implementation in many countries may be substantially improved.

Education, Health, and Nutrition

A number of other aspects of agricultural development could be discussed, such as physical infrastructure (farm-to-market roads, water-control structures), extension, credit, and other input servicing, marketing services, electricity, housing, and entertainment. Education, health, and nutrition warrant specific attention; they might appropriately be defined as human capital accumulation.

Education as a form of investment can have high payoffs, directly through the acquisition of skills that improve the income of the individual and the growth of the economy, and indirectly by raising productivity through better health, nutrition, and knowledge of and desire to practice family planning.

Adelman and Morris found that the single variable most closely associated with differences in patterns of income distribution was the rate of improvement in human resources.

> Higher school enrollment ratios are uniformly associated with less concentration in income distribution and with larger shares accruing to the lower and middle income strata. [Adelman and Morris, 1971a, p. 36]

Education is also highly valued as a consumption good that can contribute to greater enjoyment of life. Education can have the macroeconomic benefit of delaying labor-force entry. From 1951 to 1965 rising schooling rates were an important reason that Taiwan's unemployment rate declined [Ho, 1972].

On the other hand, education has often failed to make a positive contribution to development. Much educational effort in the low-income world has been modeled after colonial educational systems, which were primarily designed to funnel the brightest students into lower-level civil service positions. The consequence of rapid expansion of these systems has been an unbalanced educational output, with many school leavers who expect to secure civil service and related jobs and few technically trained graduates. Sadly but ironically, many low-income countries find themselves with very high rates of unemployment among "educated" groups, while having critical shortages of skilled people in technical fields. Both the Colombia and Sri Lanka studies concluded that the education systems were highly inappropriate to the needs of development and employment generation [ILO, 1970, 1971]. Particularly in Sri Lanka, a major *cause* of high unemployment was an education system that almost exclusively prepared pupils for white-collar jobs.

Numerous reforms have been proposed by educational specialists, including various types of "nonformal" education [Owens and Shaw, 1972, pp. 121–133]. It is certain that if living conditions of the poorest are to improve, they must acquire new agricultural, mechanical, and household skills to permit them to be productive in a basically rural environment.

Good health and proper nutrition obviously facilitate economic growth and development by contributing to the quality and productive potential of people. It is now well established that nutritional deficiency produces physically smaller individuals, lowers intelligence, and reduces resistance to disease [Belli, 1971]. Better health is also highly valued as a consumption item; it is an important aspect of human well-being and the quality of life. When per capita income is the index of development, these consumption aspects of better health go unmeasured. For example, one well-known study concluded that in Sri Lanka in the short run (fifteen to twenty years) malaria eradication was beneficial but over the longer run it had a negative effect [Barlow, 1969]. Unfortunately, "benefits" were narrowly defined as the impact on the rate of growth of per capita income. No effort was made to capture the intrinsic benefits of improved health and reduced physical and mental suffering—that is, the contributions to current and future consumption.

There is a dearth of good data on levels and trends in educational, health, and nutritional attainments in the low-income world. There can be no doubt that overall health conditions have improved dramatically since World War II due in large part to the work of the World Health Organization and other aid agencies, in cooperation with local public health programs. Overall crude death rates have been cut in half. But better health is usually the consequence of a constellation of factors in addition to health programs per se.

> Improved agriculture, by providing more and better food, decreases mortality. Better transportation, by reducing the loss of food and decreasing isolation and ignorance, leads to the same result. Improved housing decreases crowding, and the more favorable home environment reduces the spread of communicable diseases. Improved water supply for agricultural, industrial, or other uses not primarily associated with health also reduces the spread of disease. Basic education increases understanding of personal hygiene and of the causes of disease. Mass media help diffuse knowledge and ideas. [Taylor and Hall, 1967, p. 651]

Relatively little is known about the distribution of health benefits and the incidence of sickness and death by socioeconomic class, although no one doubts that the poor, particularly in rural areas, are seriously discriminated against regarding access to health services. Raulet [1970, p. 225] provides data showing that within the same rural communities in (West) Pakistan, infant mortality rates were almost three times higher among the lower four income quintiles than among the highest income quintile for women under age thirty.

Even less is known about trends in nutrition. Large-scale starvation has been averted in the post-World War II period. Nevertheless, both undernourishment (insufficient consumption of food) and malnourishment (nutritionally improper diets) are widespread throughout the low-income world. According to United Nations data, average daily intake of calories in the low-income world is only two-thirds that of the high-income world, and average daily intake of total proteins is only 60 percent of the level in the high-income world [Pokrovsky, 1970]. Turnham [1971a, pp. 73–92] presents evidence of a close relationship between income levels and levels of calorie and protein intake. Although he was not able to measure recent trends in nutritional levels among lower income groups, current nutrition is frequently so poor as to strongly suggest that incomes, food consumption, and nutrition could not have improved much—if any—in recent years.

Educational trends are also frequently difficult to ascertain. There have clearly been some major gains in recent years. On the other hand, in the early 1960s many African countries were hoping to achieve universal primary education by 1970. Despite expenditures of up to 20 percent or more of the public budget, the goal of universal primary education remains far from attainment in almost all African nations. In many, the absolute number of children *not* in school has increased. This also appears to be the case for Mexico in recent years [Flores, 1972]. Data for India indicate that illiteracy is being reduced about 1 percent per year [Myrdal, 1968, p. 1672]. However, Myrdal questions the data, both for India and most other Asian countries; he thinks they are grossly inflated, and that in reality average educational attainment in India and some other countries is improving very little.

Access to education is highly unequal; the most disadvantaged children, particularly the poorest in rural areas, have often been left out.

> Landlords who dominate Latin American economies and politics usually send their children to urban schools. Hence, those with investable funds have little interest in improving rural education. [Thiesenhusen, 1969, p. 747]

In Mexico school attendance is by law "compulsory" between the ages of six and fourteen. In fact, however, in 1967 only one-fifth of this age group attended school [Hertford, 1971, p. 9]. Moreover, the distribution of schooling is highly skewed.

> Three-quarters of urban school-age children currently enter primary schools, yet only about half in the same age group enter schools in rural areas. Eight percent of the entering rural students complete the third year of instruction, while 50 percent of urban primary students finish 3 years. Almost half (48 percent) of the rural population over 14 years old is illiterate, while the comparable figure in urban areas is 21 percent. [Hertford, 1971, p. 10]

In Brazil the unequal access to education is a major cause of income inequality. It has been determined that

> the more skewed distribution of educational attainment itself accounts for about half the observed increase in total (income) inequality over the decade. [Fishlow, 1972, p. 401]

In India in the early 1950s, 40 percent of males were literate among nonagricultural classes; 20 percent were literate among agricultural classes. Corresponding percentages for females were 17 and 4. Within the agricultural group, only 10 percent of the landless male laborers were literate, while 48 percent of the males in families who owned but did not themselves cultivate land were literate. The corresponding percentages for women were 3 and 17 [Myrdal, 1968, p. 1679]. Although literacy rates in India have improved since then, Myrdal believes the gains have been quite modest, with little or no improvement in distribution.

> Monopoly of education is—together with monopoly of ownership of land— the most fundamental basis of inequality. [Myrdal, 1970, p. 195]

In sum, the record regarding the education, health, and nutrition aspects of development appears to provide little basis for a more encouraging assessment of overall development trends in recent years.

In this chapter, recent trends in the rural development of some important areas of the low-income world were reviewed. It was suggested that the green revolution probably presents an unprecedented opportunity for developing the agricultural sectors and improving the living conditions of both rural and urban populations in much of the low-income world. Unfortunately, this considerable potential of the green revolution may be largely frustrated, primarily by the land-tenure arrangements and other social and economic conditions that in many countries effectively prevent the poorest segment of the rural population from obtaining the benefits of the green revolution. Available data indicate that incomes are already highly unequal in at least some important regions of the low-income world, and again according to available evidence, there is little reason to believe that the distribution of levels of living—and the land-tenure arrangements and other social and economic conditions that ultimately determine the distribution of levels of living—are becoming more equal in the low-income world. On the contrary, there is evidence that at least in some countries the distribution is becoming less equal. The analysis in the following chapter suggests that this may be an important obstacle to overall fertility decline and hence may seriously hinder long-term development.

chapter 4

Rural Development and Fertility Decline

In this chapter the effects of agricultural growth and rural development on fertility decline and population growth are discussed. A two-part analytical framework is presented, one part illustrating successful rural development and fertility decline, and the second part showing successful growth in agricultural output but lack of widespread development and fertility decline. In support of these models, the experiences of several important countries are examined. Finally, the overall treatment is summarized, together with a discussion of research implications.

Toward a Framework[1]

The most important features of the framework are as follows:

1. Population growth per se—whatever the rate—is not an obstacle to growth in per capita agricultural output.
2. In most low-income countries, new agricultural technology is a precondition for agricultural growth and development. In both Figure 1 and Figure 2 this is indicated by the box labeled "stream of agricultural technologies suited to local resource endowment."

---

[1] For a related approach, see Frederiksen, 1969.

3. Whether or not rural development will be widely diffused depends largely on (a) government policies and (b) domestic institutions.

4. If increased agricultural production is widely diffused so that rural incomes are rising in a fairly egalitarian manner, then a set of processes will be activated that will lead to improved living conditions and a more modern life style for most of the rural population; one consequence will be an increasing desire among a growing proportion of parents for smaller and smaller families. Spontaneous and sustained overall fertility decline will result, which can be considerably facilitated by an efficient national family planning program. In other words, development and modernization are preconditions for sustained rural fertility decline. This process of successful rural development and fertility decline is illustrated by Figure 1.

5. If, on the other hand, domestic institutions and government policies inhibit the widespread adoption of new technologies, productivity gains are likely to be limited to the small, privileged, rural subsector.[2] As a consequence, levels of living in this subsector will rise rapidly to levels comparable to "Western," "modern" life styles. But the large impoverished subsector making up the bulk of the rural population will experience little improvement in living conditions; they will be "left behind." As a result, there will be only very limited "modernization" in their life styles; they will have little desire for smaller families; there will be only a modest overall fertility decline at best. It is unlikely that a national family planning program will find much of a market for its services among the poor. This case is illustrated by Figure 2.

The central proposition emerging from this framework is that equality in the distribution of the development process and its benefits (simplified to "improved rural incomes widely diffused" in Figure 1) will lead to a more rapid modernization process among a larger proportion of families, which in turn will lead to a more widespread desire for smaller families and hence an earlier, more rapid and sustained overall fertility decline. The mechanisms implied within this framework that cause families to desire and achieve fewer births have been put forth and analyzed in basically economic terms by Leibenstein [1957], Becker [1960], Easterlin [1969], Harmon [1970], and T. Paul Schultz and colleagues [Schultz, 1969, 1971, 1972; Nerlove and Schultz, 1970; Schultz and DaVanzo, 1970]. They will only be summarized here.

---

[2] Alternatively, utilization of new technologies that are inappropriate to the prevailing resource endowment can contribute to this type of distorted development. For example, if extensive mechanization is introduced into a rural sector that has surplus unskilled labor, agriculture will move in the direction of a dual system with a highly unequal income distribution. However, it will usually again be the set of development policies and domestic institutions that are responsible for the utilization of inappropriate technologies.

Figure 1. Successful agricultural development and fertility decline

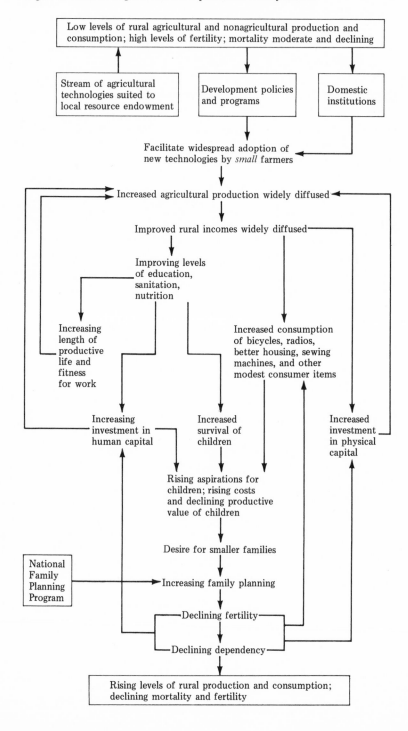

Figure 2. Successful growth in agricultural output; lack of widespread rural development and fertility decline

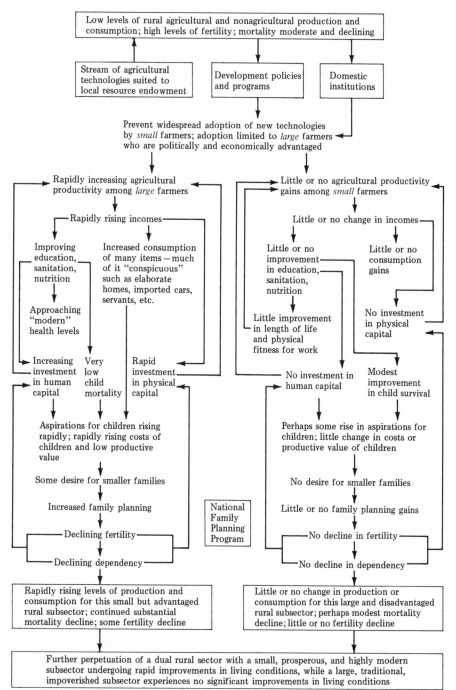

It is assumed that people are "rational" in that parents want the number of children (and the sex distribution) that they think will provide them with the greatest satisfaction or happiness. Leibenstein [1957, p. 161] distinguishes among three types of utility or satisfaction that parents derive from children: (1) as "consumption goods," that is, as a source of personal pleasure; (2) as productive resources, that is, as an eventual contributor to household income; and (3) as a potential source of security, either in old age or otherwise. Two types of costs can be distinguished. Direct costs are the expenses of maintaining the child at conventional standards until he becomes self-supporting. Indirect costs are the opportunities foregone caused by the existence of the child, such as reduced parental mobility and reduced income-earning potential of the mother. As modernization (as described earlier) takes place within the family, the changes in attitudes, values, and life styles that take place are likely to produce a decline in the *relative* importance of children as a source of satisfaction or productive value and a rise in their absolute costs (both direct and indirect)—the net effect being a desire for fewer and fewer children. Some of the specific processes through which modernization brings about these changes are described below.

First, as health conditions improve and mortality—particularly of infants—declines, fewer births are required to obtain a given number of surviving children. Although parental perception of reduced mortality may lag somewhat behind the actual decline, evidence is accumulating that indicates that declining mortality is an important cause of the desire for fewer births.

> In Puerto Rico and Taiwan, the reduction of death rates appears to have fostered the significant reduction in birth rates. In the Philippines and East Pakistan, the frequency of earlier child deaths in a family is a good predictor of further births . . . in Taiwan, . . . the loss of a child less than age 15 is associated with a rise in birth rates 3 years later more than sufficient to replace the lost child and to increase the number of children likely to survive to age 15. [Schultz, 1971, pp. 162–163]

Moreover, the uncertainty that prevails under conditions of high mortality may cause parents to aim for more births than they really desire as a hedge against possible future deaths among their children. The perception of reduced mortality would thus reduce the need for such "insurance" births and might result in an overcompensating fall in birth rates. [Schultz, 1971, p. 157]

In addition, the rising probability of surviving childhood and reaching old age increases the expected returns to education and related forms of human capital formation undertaken at early ages. Education—particularly of women and children—appears to lead universally to a desire for smaller families [Miro and Mertens, 1968; Rich, 1973]. Childhood education, even if provided free by the state, increases the costs of raising children because of the need for better clothing, school materials, transportation, and (in many cases) school fees; in addition, it reduces the contribution of children to family income since their performance of routine household chores must be curtailed. Education of women serves to expand women's opportunities for work and social interaction beyond traditional limits and thus to increase the sources of personal satisfaction and fulfillment that traditionally may have been provided primarily by childbearing and child rearing. In addition, these new alternatives increase the opportunity cost to a woman of early motherhood and large families. This may lead to a later age at marriage and a desire for smaller families. Evidence indicates that women working for wages have lower fertility than women with otherwise similar characteristics [Kasarda, 1971]. Finally, it appears universally true that educated parents value more highly educated children and generally prefer fewer children with correspondingly greater prospects of educational achievement. "It is possible, therefore, that the schooling of each generation paves the way for the increased education opportunities enjoyed by the next" [Schultz, 1969, p. 158]. Education can also be a means of obtaining birth control information and thereby it serves to reduce the cost and increase the likelihood of avoiding an unwanted birth.

A third cause of the desire for fewer children is that the modernization process generates aspirations for material possessions such as radios, bicycles, better housing, and sewing machines, as well as aspirations for savings and expenditures such as land purchases and improvements, water pumps, fertilizers, improved implements, and various other agricultural inputs that will produce larger future incomes. These items can usually be more easily acquired by those with fewer children since some additional household resources will thus be available that otherwise would have been required for the rearing of a larger family.

Finally, as the development and modernization process continues, new forms of old age security are likely to reduce the former reliance of aged parents on their children. Moreover, parents may perceive that fewer but better-educated children are likely to be better prospects for providing care in later years than a larger number of poorly-educated children.

To the extent that these processes are taking place, they will have a self-perpetuating or feedback effect: satiation of some aspirations may lead to the emergence of others, and investments undertaken earlier will produce continued increases in incomes and levels of living.

In summary, modernization usually functions to change all the above family characteristics in a direction favorable to smaller family norms. That is, modernization brings reduced mortality, higher educational enrollments and achievements, material sources of satisfaction in addition to children, less need to depend on children in one's old age, and in addition tends to be a self-reinforcing process. In the discussions of specific development experiences that follow, more examples are given of some of these relationships between modernization and the desire for smaller families.

During the period when these changes are taking place within families, easy access to family planning services will make parents better able to match their fertility behavior to their changing aspirations and hence further enhance both the modernization process itself as well as overall fertility decline. Indeed, access to effective, safe, and easy-to-use contraceptives is in its own right an important aspect of "development" and improved living conditions.

Supporting Evidence[3]

At the present time it is not possible to provide adequate statistical tests of the relationships hypothesized here between rural development and fertility decline. In the first place, even for high-income countries detailed data on the distributional aspects of development that would permit a test of these hypotheses are not available. Second, development of the appropriate statistical techniques for testing these relationships is simply beyond the scope of this paper.

It is possible, however, to examine the development experiences of several, mostly low-income, countries to see to what extent if any the hypothesized relationships can be observed. The countries that will be discussed here include the seven Asian and two Latin American countries whose income distributions were given in Tables 3.2 and 3.3 as well as India, China, Costa Rica, and the United States. In Table 4.1 the thirteen countries are divided into three groups based on their fertility experiences (columns 9 and 10). At the same time, as in Table 3.3, they are ranked according to their index of relative income inequality (column 4)—from relatively more equal to relatively less equal. At the top of the table are those countries that have experienced considerable overall fertility decline— South Korea, Japan, Taiwan, West Malaysia, and the United States. At the other extreme is the group of countries that have experienced little or no overall fertility decline—India, the Philippines, Thailand, Mexico, and Brazil. In between is the group of countries in which overall fertility decline has taken or is taking place, although it is not as well documented as for the countries in the first group. These countries are Sri Lanka, China,[4] and Costa Rica.[5] Since comparable income distribution indices are not available for China, Costa Rica, India, and the United States, they are grouped solely

---

[3] For a complementary treatment of some of the discussion that follows, see Johnston [1966] and Rich [1973].

[4] The crude birth rate estimates for China are only informed guesses since adequate data are unavailable.

[5] See Kirk [1971] for a discussion of recent fertility decline and associated economic and social characteristics in some other low-income countries.

according to their fertility experiences.[6] Table 4.1 also supplies in summary form some data on growth rates of agricultural output and population and crude birth rates for these countries.

Columns 6 and 7 indicate no systematic relationship between the rate of population growth and whether or not food production has kept pace with or exceeded population growth. Nor is there a relationship between food production and the level of per capita income. This is true both across countries and within countries for different time periods. On the other hand, as indicated by columns 4, 9, and 10, there appears to be a rather close and consistent relationship between relative income inequality and fertility trends.

In the treatment that follows, evidence from the development experiences of these countries will be used in discussing sequentially the five propositions given at the beginning of this chapter which are incorporated into the two figures.

Population Growth and Agricultural Output

The first contention is that *population growth is not an obstacle to growth in per capita agricultural output,* even in densely populated countries. Experiences from a host of countries indicate no systematic relationship between growth in agricultural output—including its capacity to keep pace with population growth—and the *rate* of population growth itself.

China and India have been densely populated for centuries. Over the last six centuries, China's population increased five- to six-fold, growing at an average annual rate of 0.4 percent. Food production increased a little faster, so that per capita food production rose slightly [Perkins, 1969]. During the last two decades, China's population has apparently grown by at least 1.5–2 percent annually. Although data on growth in aggregate food production are not available, without doubt the rate of growth in food production has at least kept pace with population growth [Orleans, 1971].

From 1700 to 1900 India's population grew at an average annual rate of about 0.3 percent, doubling from 120 to 240 million. Food shortages and severe famines occurred throughout this period. During the decade of 1891–1901 alone, about 19 million people died of starvation [Davis, 1951, p. 39]. Even so, the mortality impact of famine was considerably blunted during

---

[6] Oshima does have comparable data on income distribution in the United States for 1959. The index of income inequality was 53, or nearly identical to that of West Malaysia. It was omitted from Table 4.1 because it is not necessarily indicative of conditions that prevailed in the period of United States history being considered here, namely 1880–1940. The same criticism could be made for Japan, although since the Japanese development experience and fertility decline is more recent than that of the United States, Japan's income distribution (in 1963) may reflect somewhat more accurately the conditions that prevailed during the relevant period (and particularly during the early postwar period).

TABLE 4.1 Estimated economic, agricultural, and demographic indicators for selected countries

Country (1)	Estimated per capita income Year (2)	Dollars (3)	Relative income inequality: Sum of decile deviations from 10 percent (4)	Average annual growth (percent) Period (5)	Agricultural output (6)	Population (7)	Crude birth rate Period (8)	Beginning (9)	End (10)
Group 1									
South Korea	1961	$ 106	38	1960–70	u	2.5	1950–60	45	42
	1969	210					1960–70	42	30
Japan	1961	383	45	1880–1960	1.6	1.2	1920–55	36	19
	1969	1,430							
Taiwan	1961	116	47	1920–40	4.2	2.4	1932–47	45	41
	1969	300		1950–60	4.5	3.5	1963–70	36	26
				1960–70	4.5	2.7			
West Malaysia	1961	368	52	1958–67	u	3.0	1956–70	47	32
	1969	340							
Group 2									
United States			u	1880–1960	1.5	1.6	1880–1940	40	19
Sri Lanka	1961	123	67	1958–68	3.9	2.5	1950–70	39	32
	1969	190							
China	1961	83	u		u	u	1950–70	43	32
Costa Rica	1961	510	u		u	u	1954–69	51	32

Group 3	Year			Period			Period		
India	1961	70	u	1920–40	0.2	1.0	1920–40	46	45
	1969	110		1940–50	−1.0	1.0	1950–60	43	45
				1950–60	3.5	2.0	1960–70	45	45
				1960–67	−1.0	2.5			
				1967–71	6.0	2.5			
Philippines	1961	188	74	1902–61	2.4	2.3	1960–70	45	45
	1969	210							
Thailand	1961	101	76	1952–63	4.3	2.7	1960–70	43	43
	1969	160		1959–69	7.0	3.2			
Mexico	1961	297	82	1948–55	8.4	2.5	1950–60	44	44
	1969	580		1955–70	4.0	3.2	1960–70	44	41
Brazil	1961	268	99	1950–60	4.0	3.0	1950–60	41	41
	1969	270		1960–70	4.0	3.0	1960–70	41	38

SOURCES: For sources of columns 2 and 3, see Table 3.2; for column 4, see Table 3.3. Other sources are, by country, as follows: *South Korea*: Kim et al., 1972, pp. 3, 14, 29; U.N. 1969b, p. 260. *Japan*: Hayami and Ruttan, 1971, p. 113; Taeuber, 1958, p. 311. *Taiwan*: Christensen, 1968, p. 2; Lee and Sun, 1972, p. 29; U.N., 1949–1950, pp. 290–291. *West Malaysia*: Hardee et al., 1972, p. 137. *United States*: Hayami and Ruttan, 1971, p. 113; U.S., 1960, p. B19–36. *Sri Lanka*: ILO, 1971, vol. II, p. 6; U.N., 1969b, p. 260; U.N., 1970, p. 622. *China*: Orleans, 1971, p. 19. *Costa Rica*: U.N., 1965a, p. 282; U.N., 1970, p. 620. *India*: Sen, 1965, pp. 409–413; Abel, 1971, p. 36; Visaria, 1972, Table 10. *Philippines*: Hooley and Ruttan, 1969, p. 222; U.N., 1970, p. 623; Concepcion, 1970, p. 1. *Thailand*: Silcock, 1969, p. 124; Adulavidhaya and Prachuabmoh, 1972, p. 4; U.N., 1970, p. 622. *Mexico*: Raj, 1969, p. 17; U.N., 1969b, p. 261; U.N., 1970, p. 621. *Brazil*: Nicholls, 1971, p. 378; U.N., 1969b, p. 261; U.N., 1970, p. 621.

u = unavailable.

that period by British relief measures. From 1920 to 1950, the population was growing at about 1 percent annually. Sen [1965, pp. 410–411] reports that from 1920 to 1940, total agricultural output increased at only about 0.2 percent annually, and from 1940 to 1950 it *declined* by about 1 percent annually, implying that *per capita* output decreased by about one-third over that 30-year period. On the other hand, from 1950 to 1960, population growth accelerated to 2 percent annually while agricultural output grew at 3.5 percent annually. In the third five-year plan (1961–1966), agriculture was given a lower development priority, food production leveled off, successive monsoon failures resulted in substantial decline in output from 1965 to 1967, prices rose rapidly, and widespread famine was averted only through massive food imports. In 1965 the Indian government made agricultural development first priority, aiming for food self-sufficiency by 1972. New high-yielding varieties were introduced in 1965–1966. Total output increased from 74 million tons in 1966–1967 to 113 million tons in 1971–1972.

Within India, both agricultural and population growth have varied considerably among states. From 1952–1958 to 1964–1965, crop output grew at 3.01 percent annually in India; food-grain output increased at 2.50 percent annually. Corresponding rates of growth for Punjab state were 4.56 and 4.17 percent. Meanwhile, annual population growth averaged 2.19 percent for all India and 2.16 percent for Punjab. At the other end of the scale, in the state of Assam, crop output increased 1.17 percent annually, food-grain output increased only 0.76 percent annually, but the population grew at 3.15 percent annually [Raj, 1969, p. 26].

In Taiwan, the population growth averaged 3.4 percent annually from 1951 to 1965 [Ho, 1972, p. 218], although by 1970 it was down to 2.2 percent annually [Worth et al., 1971, p. 64]. Agricultural output grew at about 4.5 percent annually during the 1950s [Christensen, 1968].

According to official data, over the period 1959–1969 total agricultural output in Thailand increased at an average annual rate of 7.1 percent, while paddy (rice) increased at 6.8 percent annually [Adulavidhaya and Prachuab-moh, 1972, p. 4]. The Thai population was growing at about 3 percent annually [Unhanand et al., 1972, p. 2].

From 1948 to 1955, crop output increased 8.5 percent annually in Mexico; it has since increased at about 4 percent annually [Raj, 1969]. Meanwhile, population has been growing at 3 percent or more per year. On the other hand, for a long period prior to 1940, agricultural output in Mexico was stagnant, while the population was growing much more slowly. In Brazil, population growth has averaged about 3 percent per year over the past two decades, while *per capita* agricultural output has increased about 1 percent annually [Nicholls, 1971].

Over the eighty-year period, 1880–1960, Japan's population increased from 36 to 93 million, while the United States population increased from 50 to 181 million, averaging 1.15 percent annual growth in Japan and 1.6 percent in the United States. Growth in agricultural output during this period averaged 1.6 percent annually in Japan and 1.5 percent in the United States [Hayami and Ruttan, 1971, p. 113].

Many more examples could be cited, all suggesting that the capacity for agricultural output to increase as rapidly or even more rapidly than population does not appear to be in any way associated with higher or lower population growth rates. In fact, Abercrombie compared rates of growth of population, per capita incomes, and food production for thirty-three countries representing about three-quarters of the population of the low-income world —excluding China—for the period 1952–1956 to 1960–1964. He concluded that

> the density of population appears to have had little influence on the rate at which it has been possible to increase food production. . . . The highest rates of production increase have occurred in some of the countries where population growth is fastest, but equally there are a number with rapid population growth where production has lagged notably, and others where production has been expanded sharply in the absence of a rapid increase in population. The countries where production has failed to keep up with population include those with both rapid and moderate population growth. [Abercrombie, 1969, pp. 3–4]

The Role of Agricultural Technology

This leads to the second contention, namely, that in *most* low-income countries, *new agricultural technology is a precondition to agricultural growth and development.*[7] In an influential book, Schultz [1964] argued that peasant farmers were sufficiently intelligent and rational so that for all practical purposes each had organized his land, labor, skills, and other inputs into an economically optimum combination, given the technology at his disposal. That is, through the centuries the *best* agricultural methods had survived and been refined.[8] Given the constraints farmers faced, there was no way they could improve their living conditions; peasant farmers the world over were, in effect, intelligent and rational within the confines of traditional agriculture. Schultz defined a "traditional agriculture" as one that has achieved a long-range equilibrium representing the most efficient allocation of productive resources actually available to farmers. If farmers trapped

---

[7] In many parts of the world, rapid increases in agricultural output have been achieved with apparently little or no use of new technology, usually because unused but potentially productive lands could be exploited with existing technology. This opportunity has already been exhausted in many places and will probably eventually be exhausted in all or nearly all countries.

[8] "Best" here means the combination of crop varieties and cultivation methods that produces the greatest return, given the skills of the cultivator, certain subjective considerations such as various kinds of risk (weather, pests) and tastes, and the trade-offs between work and other activities.

within a traditional agriculture were to be transformed so as to become rational with respect to modern agriculture, new, superior technologies that would induce farmers to modernize had to be made available from sources *outside* the agrarian structure itself.

The response of farmers in the last few years to the new biological technology and its complementary inputs has validated Schultz's thesis. In many low-income rural areas the technology constraint has been broken and farmers have been provided with sufficient economic incentives so that they have augmented and altered the combination of their inputs and dramatically increased their production. By combining the new seeds with a whole "package" of additional modern inputs—fertilizers, tube wells, insecticides and pesticides, credit, sophisticated farming practices (planting depths and densities, harvesting practices), and so forth—farmers have been induced to abandon traditional for modern agriculture.

All the success stories of the current green revolution can be traced to this source. Although extension of cultivated area in Mexico contributed to the phenomenal expansion of crop output there in the late 1940s and early 1950s, the introduction of new higher-yielding varieties provided the technological potential and incentive. Grain yields in most of Asia and particularly in India were very low prior to the green revolution.

> During the 1961–63 period, average grain yields were less than one-fourth those in most advanced countries such as Japan or the United Kingdom. Grain yields, though showing a tendency to rise in recent years, have changed very little over the 6-decade period for which data are available. [Brown, 1965, p. 27]

For example, in the Philippines output per land area actually declined in the 1902–1960 period [Hooley and Ruttan, 1969, p. 248]. Rice yields in Thailand declined almost continuously over several decades prior to 1960 [Silcock, 169, p. 122]. Almost all the increase in total agricultural output in both the Philippines and Thailand has been the result of extending the acreage cultivated. However, at least in Thailand, little potential now remains for increasing output by cultivating new lands, "because little unused agricultural land of good quality now remains" [Adulavidhaya and Prachuab-moh, 1972, p. 25].

> Speaking about South-East Asia, the phenomenon of the low rate of growth in agricultural production till 1964 was pervasive—exceptions like Taiwan were non-typical. And after 1965, when the breakthrough began to occur, it was shared by most of the countries. In both periods, these countries were pursuing diverse economic and political policies, and yet, in all these countries, they produced almost identical results, stagnation before 1964, and breakthrough thereafter. [Dantwala, 1970, p. 5]

New agricultural technology—especially biological—has also been a primary source of many earlier agricultural success stories. In Taiwan in the pre-World War II period, the Japanese introduced higher-yielding varieties along with the supporting rural infrastructure of irrigation, transportation, research, extension, and marketing facilities. In the period from 1926 to 1970, rice yields per hectare more than doubled [Lee and Sun, 1972, p. 15]. The Japanese carried out a similar though more modest agricultural development effort in Korea during the 1920s and 1930s. As in Japan and Taiwan, Korean agricultural productivity has increased rapidly. In 1920 rice yields were 1.0 to 1.5 tons per hectare; in 1970 average yields were 3.0 to 3.5 tons per hectare [Park, 1972, p. 3]. There is evidence that in China as far back as 1000 A.D. superior rice varieties were propagated whose chief advantages apparently were drought resistance and shorter ripening periods, thereby permitting double cropping [Dalrymple, 1972, p. 52]. In Japan, farmland increased only 28 percent from 1880 to 1960, but yields per hectare almost tripled. Throughout this period, increased productivity was the consequence of a stream of labor- and land-intensive agricultural technologies, especially the use of higher-yielding varieties [Hayami and Ruttan, 1971]. On the other hand, because frontier land existed in the United States until the early twentieth century, agricultural expansion up to that time was the result of land extension and mechanization. From 1880 to 1920 the area farmed increased 150 percent, and a constant stream of labor-saving machines were introduced. Yields per acre actually declined 28 percent during that period. However, by 1920 the frontier had been eliminated. United States agriculture became increasingly land intensive over the next forty years as yields per acre doubled, largely because of new biological technologies produced by public research institutions [Hayami and Ruttan, 1971].

This is not to argue that there are no other important determinants of agricultural growth. Physical infrastructure is very important, and in most countries governments must either provide it or assist farmers in acquiring it. In many countries irrigation works are of special importance. A feature common to Mexico, Taiwan, and the Indian Punjab—a success story discussed later—is that

> they had not only considerable irrigation facilities as a result of past investments but there was extension of irrigated area during the period in which high rates of growth were recorded. [Raj, 1969, p. 34]

Johnson notes that those higher-income countries that have been most successful in developing their agricultural sectors

> have encouraged agricultural production with publicly supported biological, chemical and mechanical research. . . . Further, the farmers in these countries have been supplied with roads, technical assistance, markets, schools, pest protection, disease prevention services, etc. [Johnson, 1969, p. 11]

Appropriate economic incentives are also necessary in order to elicit from farmers rapid growth in output. But these necessary complementary conditions in no way detract from the essential role of new agricultural technology.

In a recent and largely original analysis of the conditions leading to agricultural change, Boserup [1965] has argued that, historically at least, rising population pressure has been the primary source of increased agricultural productivity, or more accurately, land-saving agricultural innovations that increase output per land unit. There is ample evidence from all parts of the world and over periods of many centuries to suggest that population growth has been an important cause of the shift from land-extensive to ever more land-intensive forms of agriculture. But this type of agricultural change is more appropriately termed "agricultural evolution" rather than agricultural development. For most of human history this type of agricultural change has *not* been accompanied by greater output per worker or by materially improved levels of living. In fact, output per hour worked usually declined. Further, modernization—meaning the replacement of traditional with more modern life styles and social forms and norms—has not come about.

This seems particularly well illustrated by comparing Java and Japan during the past 150 years, a comparison discussed by both Boserup [1965] and Geertz [1963]. Both societies experienced high rates of population growth and both moved a considerable distance along the agricultural evolution ladder. Java's population apparently increased from 7 million in 1830 to 42 million in 1930 to 62 million in 1960. Japan's population increased from 25 million in 1830 to 64 million in 1930 to 100 million in 1970. But one of the critical differences between Japan and Java—noted by Geertz [1963, pp. 113, 133]—is that Japanese farmers adopted practices that increased *labor* productivity as well as land productivity. Both the demand for food from outside the agricultural sector and the availability of new technologies that raised agricultural labor productivity were probably responsible. Both were absent in Java. The end result was development, modernization, and fertility decline in Japan and their absence in Java— albeit with rapid population growth and ever more land-intensive cultivation. Clearly, rapid population growth is not a sufficient condition for agricultural development and modernization, although at least historically, under some circumstances it may have been a necessary condition.

The Role of Policies and Institutions

The third contention is that once appropriate new technologies are available, *whether or not rural development will be widely diffused depends largely on (a) government policies and (b) domestic institutions.* It is clear that rapid growth in agricultural output can take place either in small-scale agriculture as in Japan and Taiwan or in large-scale agriculture as in much of Mexico, Brazil, and the United States. Over the past thirty years, Mexican agriculture has developed along highly dualistic lines, and the spectacular gains in output have been concentrated among a fairly small group of progressive, large-scale, prosperous farmers in the north and Pacific north regions [Raj, 1969]. By 1957, 95 percent of the country's cotton and almost

70 percent of the wheat, the two crops whose production expanded most, were grown in seven northern states containing less than one-third of the total rural population. Living conditions for perhaps two-thirds of the total rural population of over 20 million have improved little and for some may have deteriorated. This situation has resulted, on the one hand, from development policies of the Mexican government that encouraged large-scale, mechanized, highly commercial agriculture, and on the other hand, from the pattern of land ownership, which consists of a small group of very large landowners, particularly in the less densely populated and more productive north and northwest, together with very small private or communal (*ejido*) holdings—generally on less productive land—for the bulk of the rural population. These two factors have produced what may be one of the most unequal income distributions in the world. Overall, Mexico has a highly unequal pattern of income distribution, but, as was noted earlier, incomes are far less equally distributed in the rural areas, where they average half the level of urban incomes, while the incomes of the rural top 5 percent are as high as those of the urban top 5 percent.[9]

Brazilian agriculture is characterized by small-scale, largely sharecropper farming in the north and large-scale mechanized hired-worker agriculture in the south. Again it has been the combination of government development policy and the prevailing distribution of land ownership that has produced a highly dualistic agriculture. And again, the result has been a sharply skewed rural income distribution. Although agriculture is considerably more productive and profitable in the south, permanently hired workers (including sharecroppers), who comprise the bulk of the rural population in both

---

[9] The benefits of the Mexican land reform in terms of social justice to the rural poor should not be underestimated, however. In 1910 before the reforms began, of about 4 million Mexican farm workers, only 3 percent owned land [Hertford, 1971, p. 35]. Since 1917 literally millions of rural Mexicans have escaped servitude and enjoyed a degree of personal freedom that was unthinkable earlier. Moreover, *ejido* production of both food and cash crops has expanded rapidly and as a consequence, the level of living of the average *ejidatario* (*ejido* farmer) is no doubt considerably higher than it would have been in the absence of the reforms. But for several reasons the reforms have fallen far short of their potential, in particular because the land parcels acquired by the *ejidatarios* were small, the quality of the land was low (expropriated owners retained the best land), and the *ejidatarios* generally lacked technical and managerial skills and access to credit. And importantly, very large, mechanized, commercial, highly productive farms were permitted to continue to expand rapidly, particularly in the sparsely populated north and northwest as new, highly productive lands were opened through major public irrigation projects. For example, despite continued land redistribution, the number of farms in excess of 1,000 hectares increased from 16,825 in 1940 to 22,600 in 1960 [Hertford, 1971, p. 39]. As a consequence, while the absolute income levels of *ejidatarios* have probably risen modestly over the last thirty years, *ejidatarios* have been largely excluded from the enormous growth in total income and wealth in Mexico during this period. Furthermore, the prevailing rural development policies and the distribution of education and other means of human development help perpetuate the existing inequalities.

north and south, fare little better in the south than in the north and are worse off in relative terms. The average net income (including interest income) of farm-operator families in the south of Brazil was US$6,833 or seventeen times as large as the average annual family income of all their permanent hired workers ($399). Corresponding average incomes for the same two categories in the northeast were $1,642 and $205 [Nicholls, 1971, pp. 385–386].

The International Labour Organization team that produced a full-employment development strategy for Colombia contended that the prevailing distribution of land ownership is the major obstacle to better utilization of rural labor and rapid growth in agricultural output [ILO, 1970]. Thiesenhusen [1971b] believes that this can be generalized to most of Latin America.

Green revolution breakthroughs appear to be encouraging a similar pattern of rural development in much of India and Pakistan. In those areas of India where the new technology is highly profitable, some land values have risen three- to five-fold. Under circumstances of highly unequal land ownership, this has resulted in further concentration of land rights.

> Not only have rents risen from the traditional (though illegal under reforms) 50/50 to as high as 70 percent of the crop, but security of tenure and other rights in land a tenant might claim have also been perceptibly weakened. [Ladejinsky, 1970, p. 764]

It was earlier noted that sharecropping and other forms of tenancy that require farmers to turn over about half of their crops to landlords (many absentee) typify those Southeast Asian countries with less equal income distributions and slower rates of growth of agricultural output and national income [Oshima, 1970, p. 25].

Government policies and institutions, however, can facilitate both growth in agricultural output and equality in its distribution. In Japan and Taiwan, post-World War II land reforms produced an agricultural sector of very small holders, stimulated growth in agricultural output, and permitted a relatively egalitarian distribution of rural incomes. As recently as the mid-1960s, half the population of Taiwan was agricultural [FAO, 1967, p. 19]. Only 13 percent of Taiwan's farmers cultivate as much as 5 acres, while the remainder work an average of 2.6 acres [Mueller, 1971, p. 27].

> This breakup of farms into smaller units apparently was a way of improving incentives to use land more intensively and of obtaining additional agricultural production from available labor. [Christensen, 1968, p. 40]

Publicly supported research efforts contributed to this pattern of development by producing new biological technologies consistent with small-scale, labor-intensive agriculture. A similar process has taken place in South Korean agriculture.

The land-distribution policy of the United States government in the nineteenth century permitted even families with very limited resources to become landowners. Despite its rapid commercialization during this century, United States agriculture has continued to be characterized by family farms. Most farmers own a large portion of the land they farm and receive income not only from their labor but also from their property and management skills. One result was that incomes within agriculture remained relatively equally distributed during the process of rapid modernization in the late nineteenth and early twentieth centuries.

Equal Distribution and Fertility Decline

Of course, the most crucial question still remains: What is the differential impact of these contrasting patterns of agricultural growth and development on fertility? The fourth contention is that *if rural development is distributed widely and fairly equally, one important consequence will be sustained overall fertility decline.*

This contention has some features in common with the so-called Threshold Hypothesis [see United Nations, 1963, pp. 134–151; and Kirk, 1971, pp. 138–145; for a related discussion, see Rich, 1973]. According to this hypothesis, "in a developing country where fertility is initially high, improving economic and social conditions are likely to have little if any effect on fertility until a certain economic and social level is reached; but once that level is achieved, fertility is likely to enter a decided decline and to continue downward until it is again stabilized on a much lower plane" [United Nations, 1963, p. 143]. There is, however, an important difference between contention four above and this usual formulation of the Threshold Hypothesis. Contention four focuses specifically on distributional aspects of social and economic development and their effects on fertility. Treatment of the Threshold Hypothesis is generally in terms of aggregate economic and social indicators and associated fertility levels, with little or no attention to the underlying distributions. Some variables are usually included that may partially reflect the underlying distributions (for example, literacy rates, infant mortality rates, life expectancies), but even these can conceal the underlying relative equality or inequality (for example, two countries with the same overall infant mortality rate could have very different infant mortality rates for similar sub-groups in each population). Most variables provide no clues to distribution at all (for example, per capita income, urbanization, percent non-agricultural employment).[10]

---

[10] Among the other variables included in the United Nations and Kirk analyses are the following: energy consumption per capita, hospital beds, telephones, cinema attendance, newspaper circulation, and radios. It might appear that some of these provide information about the underlying distributions, but this is not necessarily the case. For example, in comparing two countries, the one with the largest number of hospital beds

The 1963 United Nations study was not very successful in being able to specify threshold values for the low-income world taken as a whole. However, when Kirk limited the analysis to regional groupings, he found some significant correlations between levels of crude birth rates and eight selected social and economic indicators, particularly for Latin America [Kirk, 1971, pp. 138–143]. It appears that at least in some cases threshold analysis may have some predictive value. For example, around 1962, four Latin American countries were within the threshold ranges for at least five of the eight variables (Guyana with 7 of the 8, Costa Rica with 6 of the 8, and Jamaica and Venezuela with 5 of the 8). According to Kirk's analysis, these were the four most likely prospects for fertility decline in Latin America in the subsequent period. In fact, both Jamaica and Costa Rica did experience fertility decline in the past decade, and fertility may have started to decline in Guyana [Kirk, p. 141]. The Costa Rican case is discussed in more detail later in this section.

However, it is the thesis of this paper that if adequate data were available from the low-income world on both fertility and a number of distributional indicators—for example, income distribution, employment, education at all levels and by all income groups, health services by social and economic groups, participation of women in education and employment—when countries at similar aggregate economic levels (for example, per capita income) were compared, analysis would produce high correlations between (a) the degree of social and economic equality and (b) the level of fertility and its rate of decline. That is, for countries at similar aggregate economic levels, the more equal the social and economic distribution, the lower would be the overall fertility level and the more rapid the fertility decline. It is further suggested that this relationship would hold true even within the rural sector. Unfortunately, as pointed out earlier, data on distributional aspects of development are scanty and it is not yet possible to extend the Threshold analysis in this way to correlate distribution indicators of development with fertility for a sufficiently large number of low-income countries. However, in this and the following section an attempt is made to examine the experiences of a few countries for which some information is available to see to what extent these relationships might exist. Below, experiences relevant to the fourth contention are examined; that is, if rural development is distributed widely and fairly equally, one important consequence will be sustained overall fertility decline.

Taiwan is perhaps the most interesting case of all. Per capita income in

per 1,000 population may have either (a) greater dispersion and a better distribution of health services (better access for the poor, implying greater equality) or (b) a greater concentration of health services among the relatively well-off segment of the population and therefore greater inequality in access to health services. In fact, the country with the lower overall rate could effectively be providing more beds per 1,000 poor people than the country with the higher overall rate.

Taiwan was only US$300 in 1969. Nonetheless, Taiwan's crude birth rate, which was in the low 40s per thousand in the prewar and early postwar periods, had declined to 27 per thousand by 1970 [Worth et al., 1971, p. 64]. Despite an age distribution that is becoming increasingly unfavorable to a continued decline in the birth rate (that is, the large postwar birth cohorts are now coming into their prime childbearing years), during 1971 the crude birth rate declined another 5 percent from 27.2 to 25.6 per thousand [Taiwan Provincial Department of Health, 1971]. Taiwan's family planning program actually began only in 1964 and became a sizable program only in 1966, but fertility began declining much earlier. Thus, although the family planning program has no doubt facilitated the fertility decline in recent years, the precipitating causes clearly lie elsewhere.

Despite a comparatively low per capita income, rural Taiwan has experienced rapid growth in agricultural output, a relatively equal distribution of rural living conditions, and fertility decline. By the 1960s the rural sector in Taiwan had experienced considerable modernization, which was relatively equally distributed. However, its origins go back to the early part of this century. In 1902–1903 the Japanese carried out a land tax reform that expropriated the land of the most powerful landlords and gave ownership to many peasant farmers. Nevertheless, tenancy remained high. A land survey in 1920–1921 showed that 42 percent of rural households were pure tenants and only 37 percent owned all the land they cultivated.

> The prevailing land tenure system gave tenants little security to their land. Rents were very high, ranging between 40 and 60 percent of the harvest . . . nearly all landlord-tenant contracts rested upon oral agreement. Such arrangements could be broken easily. Landlords picked and discarded their tenants every other year. [Myer, 1969, pp. 44–45]

In the 1920s and 1930s, the Japanese enforced measures that provided tenants with longer-term leases, written contracts, and much greater security of tenure. Finally, a thorough land reform was implemented in the early 1950s.

> The reform provided first, that tenant rents were to be reduced to 37 percent of the harvest; second, that government land was to be sold to tenants and part-owners; and finally, that landlords were to relinquish all land over a prescribed maximum (ranging from 0.5 to 2 hectares for paddy land, and 1 to 4 hectares for nonpaddy land, depending upon the class of land) at a fixed price to the government, which then sold this land to farmers. . . . The program led to a transformation of the old land tenure system. In 1950, 40 percent of rural households were tenants, 33 percent owned their farms, and the remainder were part-owners. By 1956 only 17 percent were tenants, 60 percent were owners, and 23 percent were part-owners. By 1965 the proportions were 13, 67, and 20 percent respectively, indicating the continuing influence of the reforms. [Myers, 1969, pp. 45–46]

Output has grown rapidly in Taiwan's small-holder agriculture and the resulting improvements in living conditions have had an antinatalist effect. Rural fertility has declined about as rapidly as urban fertility; from 1964 to 1969 the total fertility rate declined 20.4 percent in cities and 17.4 percent in rural areas [Lee and Sun, 1972, p. 23]. This is primarily because people's aspirations have risen as a consequence of modernization and improved living conditions.

> The new aspirations for Taiwanese farmers include new tastes for modern consumer goods and services, but they encompass other goals as well. They include a desire for modern educated children who will be able to leave farming for urban occupations, a felt need for farm equipment and other modern farm inputs, and a felt need for the savings necessary to achieve these goals. . . . Agricultural development is altering the attitudes of farmers toward the economics of family size. [Mueller, 1971, p. 5]

These new aspirations increase the burden of raising children and cause parents to want smaller families. Taiwan's family planning program has contributed to the declining rural fertility by providing good access to family planning services. About 37 percent of farm families practice contraception. Family planning is positively associated with education; 29 percent of the farmers with the least schooling practice contraception, and the rate rises to 40 percent for those who have gone beyond primary school. Ideal family size is negatively related to income.

> [T]he kinds of farmers to whom the labor of their children should be most valuable—those with the larger and more productive farms—want, if anything, smaller families than others. The most obvious interpretation is that for farmers in Taiwan, because of the small size of land holdings, children have sharply diminishing utility as productive agents after the second, and perhaps already the first, son. [Mueller, 1971, p. 21]

An additional factor that no doubt has made an important contribution to fertility decline in Taiwan is the good health the population now enjoys. In 1971 Taiwan's crude death rate was 4.9 per thousand.

> The island is almost free of communicable diseases, with the TB rate one-tenth of what it was twenty years ago, with polio almost eradicated, and even the dreaded Japanese B encephalitis at a new low level. [Keeny, 1972, p. 6]

Somewhat earlier, Japan experienced a similar fertility decline. Table 4.2 shows that in the thirty-five-year period from 1920 to 1955, the crude birth rate was almost cut in half. Fertility, as indicated by gross reproduction rates, declined by at least 50 percent over this period in both nonagricultural and agricultural areas (Hokkaido is a predominantly agricultural island). Note

TABLE 4.2   Fertility and population growth in Japan, 1920–1955

Year	Crude birth rate	Crude death rate	Rate of natural increase	Gross reproduction rates					
				All Japan	Metro-politan	Other indus-trial	Inter-mediate	Agri-cultural	Hok-kaido
1920	36.1	24.4	10.7	u	u	u	u	u	u
1925	34.8	20.3	14.5	2.6	2.1	2.4	2.6	2.8	3.1
1930	32.4	18.2	14.2	2.4	1.9	2.1	2.4	2.7	2.9
1935	31.7	16.8	14.9	u	u	u	u	u	u
1940	29.4	16.4	13.0	u	u	u	u	u	u
1947	u	u	u	2.2	1.8	2.0	2.2	2.3	2.4
1950	28.1	10.9	17.2	1.8	1.5	1.7	1.8	2.0	2.3
1955	19.3	7.8	11.6	1.2	0.9	1.0	1.2	1.4	1.4

SOURCE: Taeuber, 1958, pp. 246 and 311.
u = unavailable.

that the greatest fall in the crude birth rate and fertility rates was in the postwar period. The overall crude birth rate declined from 29 in 1940 and 28 in 1950 to 19 in 1955. Similarly, the overall gross reproduction rate fell from 2.4 in 1930 and 2.2 in 1947 to 1.2 in 1955. For agricultural areas, the gross reproduction rate fell from 2.7 in 1930 and 2.3 in 1947 to 1.4 in 1955. Corresponding rates for Hokkaido were 2.9, 2.4, and 1.4. Tsuchiya [1972, p. 39] reports more recent data indicating that by 1965 fertility levels were almost identical in rural and urban areas; total fertility was 2.19 in rural areas and 2.13 in urban areas.

A dramatic fertility decline took place between 1947 and 1955, associated with an income distribution that apparently became more egalitarian following the war and during the subsequent economic boom, particularly in rural Japan.[11] Immediately following the war, a drastic land reform was implemented. Only 30 percent of farm families owned their own land before the war; as a consequence of the land reform the percentage was 62 in 1950 and 75 in 1966 [Fukutake, 1972, table 4]. The percentage of farmers who were tenants (owning no land) declined from 29 in 1940 to 5 in 1950 and 3 in 1960.

The story in South Korea is similar, though more recent. Although South Korea's per capita income was only US$210 in 1969, during the 1960s the crude birth rate fell from 42 to 30 per thousand [Kim et al., 1972, pp. 175–179]. Table 4.3 shows that from 1960 to 1968 the total fertility rate declined 26 percent in rural areas while declining 30 percent overall. It is important to note that South Korea has a more equal income distribution than any of the

---

[11] In the immediate postwar period, the fertility rate was somewhat inflated, however, by a baby boom. The precipitous fertility decline following the baby boom was greatly facilitated by the enactment in 1948 of the Eugenic Protection Law, which provided virtually unlimited access to legal abortion.

TABLE 4.3   Nationwide and rural fertility levels in South Korea, 1960–1968

| Age group | Age-specific fertility rate[a] | | | | Indices: 1968 as a percent of 1960 | |
| | Nationwide | | Rural | | | |
	1960	1968	1960	1968	Nationwide	Rural
15–19	30	7	36	8	23	22
20–24	267	146	292	178	55	61
25–29	323	301	331	305	93	92
30–34	264	201	278	220	76	79
35–39	204	120	220	147	59	67
40–44	108	65	109	87	60	80
45–49	18	7	21	11	39	52
Total fertility rate[b]	6,070	4,235	6,435	4,780	70	74

SOURCE: Youn Keun Cha, 1972, Table 4, p. 11.

[a] Total number of children born in the specific year per thousand women in the given age group.

[b] Approximately equivalent to the total number of children born per thousand women during their reproductive life. Specifically, it indicates the total number of children 1,000 women would bear if they passed through their reproductive years with the age-specific fertility of a particular year.

other countries listed in Tables 4.1 and 4.2. Moreover, in the late 1960s, rural incomes—when adjusted to cost of living differences—compared quite favorably to urban wage incomes [Kim, 1971, p. 12]. South Korean agriculture also is characterized by very small holdings, high-yielding crop varieties, and labor-intensive practices. Average farm size has decreased from 1.17 hectares in 1920–1925 to 0.87 hectares (about 2 acres) in 1965–1970 [Park, 1972, p. 1].

South Korea's family planning program was inaugurated officially in 1962 and began effective operation in 1964. But there is evidence that fertility had been declining earlier as a consequence of delayed marriage and greater use of birth control within marriage. From 1925 to 1960 average age at marriage rose about 6½ years for both men and women [Kim et al., 1972, p. 14]. From 1935–1939 to 1965–1968, average age at marriage for women rose from 16.7 to 23.0 in urban areas and from 15.8 to 22.0 in rural areas [Cha, 1972, p. 3]. Contraceptive practice appears to be as high or higher in rural than in urban areas. Although it is difficult to determine the extent to which the family planning program has been responsible for the fertility decline, apparently the most accepted estimate is that the program caused a reduction in the crude birth rate of about 10 percent or only about one-third of the total decline [Kim et al., 1972, pp. 162–163, 169–170].

While descriptions of the distributional pattern of rural development in West Malaysia (formerly Malaya) are not available, in Tables 3.3 and 4.1

TABLE 4.4   Estimated fertility rates per thousand women, by area of residence, West Malaysia, 1959 and 1967

Residence[a]	Total fertility rate		Percent change: 1959–1967
	1959	1967	
Total population	6,055	5,230	−13.6
Metropolitan towns	5,615	3,970	−29.3
Towns	5,465	4,065	−25.6
Urbo-rural	5,600	5,720	+ 2.1
Rural areas	6,270	5,690	− 9.3

SOURCE: Hardee, Matzuki, Tan Boon Ann, and Hew Wai Sin, 1972, Table 10, p. 139.

[a] "Metropolitan towns" include all state capitals and those cities having a population of more than 75,000 in the 1959 census; "Towns" are places with a population of 7,670–75,000 in the 1959 census; "Urbo-rural areas" are those areas that do not fall into either of the two categories above but have urban characteristics and where those dependent on nonagricultural occupation are likely to be more than 60 percent of the total population; and "Rural areas" are all other areas.

West Malaysia is among the group of countries with a relatively equal income distribution. West Malaysia's crude birth rate has been declining continuously since 1956, although a national family planning program was started only in 1966–1967. From 1956 to 1970 the crude birth rate declined 31 percent, from 46.7 to 32.1 per thousand [Hardee et al., 1972, pp. 137–138]. From 1959 to 1969 the total fertility rate for the entire population declined 21.3 percent. Data differentiating the decline in total fertility by residence are available only for 1959–1967 and are presented in Table 4.4. They show that while the greatest decline was in towns and cities, total fertility in rural areas declined 9.3 percent during this eight-year period as compared to 13.6 percent for the whole of West Malaysia.

Data are unavailable on income distribution in the United States during the period 1880–1940, although Kuznets [1955, pp. 7–8] believes that during the late nineteenth and early twentieth century incomes were distributed somewhat more equally in the rural than in the urban sector. It was suggested earlier that the family farm, together with the high proportion of owner-operator farmers that has characterized United States agriculture, facilitated a rapid growth in agricultural production and a relatively equal distribution of rural incomes. By 1880 the overall crude birth rate in the United States had apparently declined substantially; it may have been as high as 55 per thousand at the beginning of the nineteenth century. Nevertheless, Table 4.5 shows that the crude birth rate of 40 per thousand in 1880 was cut in half in the following sixty-year period. According to the only available indicator for comparing rural and urban fertility levels—number of children under age five per thousand women age twenty to forty-four—by 1940 fertility in both urban and rural areas had declined to about two-thirds their 1910 levels.

Evidence of dramatic fertility decline in two other countries—China and

TABLE 4.5   Fertility and population growth in the United States, 1880–1940

	Crude birth rate		Crude death rate		Rate of natural increase		Number of children under age 5 per 1,000 white women 20–44 years old		
Year	Total	White	Total	White	Total	White	Total	Rural	Urban
1880	39.8	35.1	u	u	u	u	u	u	u
1890	u	31.5	u	u	u	u	u	u	u
1900	32.3	30.1	17.2	17.0	15.1	13.1	u	u	u
1910	30.1	29.2	14.7	14.5	15.4	14.7	609	782	469
1920	27.7	26.9	13.0	12.6	14.7	14.3	581	744	471
1930	21.3	20.6	11.3	10.8	10.0	9.8	485	658	388
1940	19.4	18.6	10.8	10.4	8.6	8.2	400	551	311

SOURCE: United States, 1960, pp. B 19–36, B 37–91, and B 129–142.
u = unavailable.

Costa Rica—has stirred international interest. Although adequate data are not available to indicate the extent of fertility decline in China, Orleans [1971] estimates that the crude birth rate may have declined from 43 per thousand in the late 1940s to about 32 per thousand in 1970, and a number of reliable observers report widespread practice of family planning and substantial fertility decline in rural as well as urban areas [Faundes and Luukkainen, 1972]. This apparent fertility decline has been associated with dramatic improvements in living conditions for the bulk of the rural population (which still comprises an estimated 80 percent of the total population). It appears that the current regime has made considerable progress toward achieving their goal of an equal income distribution. Moreover, the success of the rural Chinese health program, including the accomplishments of the "barefoot doctors," has achieved international recognition.

The crude birth rate in Costa Rica apparently declined dramatically during the 1960s, starting from one of the highest rates in the world. It was reported as 51.4 per thousand in 1954 and 32.4 per thousand in 1969 [United Nations, 1965a, p. 282; 1970, p. 620]. Although detailed data are not yet available, it is clear that some of the decline has been in the rural sector since in 1963, 65 percent of the population was rural [United Nations, 1967, p. 23].

Costa Rica has always prided itself in being a country of small farmers [Hill, 1964, p. 44]. The landlord system that characterized most of Latin America during the past three centuries was absent from Costa Rica until the latter part of the nineteenth century when larger-than-family farms came into existence in conjunction with the production and export of coffee. While the distribution of landholdings [see United States, 1970, p. 227] suggests far greater land concentration and inequality in farm size and ownership than, for example, in Japan and Taiwan, landholdings are probably less concentrated in Costa Rica than in any other mainland Latin American country. Additional important factors are levels of education and health. Costa Rica has one of the highest levels of educational and health attainment in all of Latin America. In 1963, 95 percent of the urban population and more than 80 percent of the rural population over ten years of age were literate. In urban areas over 90 percent of children ages seven to twelve were attending school, and the percentage in rural areas was about 80 [United Nations, 1967, pp. 89–97]. Life expectancy at birth is estimated to be in the high sixties, exceeded only by that of Argentina among mainland Latin American countries [Keyfitz, 1971, p. 677].

Thus, although Costa Rica has a per capita income about equivalent to that of Mexico, the lower concentration of landholdings, the much higher literacy rate, and the better health conditions suggest that incomes and levels of living are more evenly distributed in Costa Rica than in Mexico, both overall and within the rural sector. It seems likely that a larger proportion of the population in Costa Rica than in Mexico have participated in and benefited from development and experienced some "modernization" of their lives.

Unequal Distribution and Absence of Fertility Decline

In the countries discussed above, substantial fertility decline has been associated with rapid growth in agricultural output and a relatively equal distribution of rural incomes. On the other hand, the fifth contention is that *if rapid agricultural growth takes place only in a highly commercial enclave sector, while the bulk of the rural population do not experience rising incomes and levels of living, significant overall fertility decline will not take place.*

Mexican agricultural output has been growing at more than 4 percent annually for twenty-five years; in 1969 Mexico had a per capita income of US$580; more than half the population are urban. Yet the crude birth rate had not declined by 1960 and the decline during the 1960s was quite modest—from about 44 to 41 per thousand [United Nations, 1970, p. 621]. Mexico's highly dualistic agricultural sector and grossly unequal income distribution have already been noted. Some people have argued that the Church's opposition to family planning, along with (until recently) the Mexican government's enthusiasm for a rapidly growing population, account for the lack of significant fertility decline. Yet many historic examples demonstrate that fertility can fall dramatically despite government and religious opposition—for example, France, Italy (fertility rates in northern Italy are among the lowest in the world), pre-World War II Japan, and several cities in Latin America today.

Brazil, at US$270, has a per capita income about half that of Mexico. Brazil and Mexico have similar patterns of a dualistic agricultural sector coupled with a highly unequal income distribution. Land ownership is even more skewed in Brazil than in India since

> 81.3 percent of the nonpublic land is held by 12.6 percent of the land-owners in latifundia of 1,000 to 100,000 hectares. Dwarf units fragment the other 18.7 percent of the territory among 87.4 percent of the owners. [Foland, 1969, p. 109]

As with Mexico, the overall crude birth rate had not declined prior to 1960 and the decline during the 1960s was only from about 41 to 38 per thousand [United Nations, 1969b, p. 261; 1970, p. 621], about the same amount as the Mexican decline. As in Mexico, there is no evidence of a trend toward sustained overall fertility decline. It should be recognized that both countries have sizable and growing upper and middle classes. It is to be expected that if these groups are practicing fertility limitation—as Daly [1970] argues they do—there should be some dampening effect on the overall crude birth rate. The apparently modest decline in the overall crude birth date during the 1960s in both Mexico and Brazil provides little or no basis for hoping that fertility has been reduced among either the rural or the urban poor.

In India the crude birth rate apparently rose from the 1941–1951 decade to the 1951–1961 decade. Visaria [1972, table 10] has estimated that the crude birth rates for these two decades were 42.6 and 44.9 per thousand. India has had an official national family planning program since 1952. With the implementation of the fourth five-year plan (1966–1971), the government began to promote family planning more aggressively. Although considerable effort has been made since, it is unclear whether there has been an impact on the overall crude birth rate [Visaria, 1972, pp. 43–44].

It is revealing, however, to look at the Punjab, agriculturally and demographically the most advanced state in India. From 1951–1954 to 1958–1961 the annual rate of growth of agricultural output was 5.14 percent, the highest among all states and about 50 percent higher than in the country as a whole [Visaria, 1972, p. 47]. This differential has widened since the introduction of new seed varieties. In 1969–1970, 70 percent of the Punjab wheat land was planted to high-yielding varieties; in Ludhiana district alone, the figure was 97.2 percent [Visaria, 1972, p. 7].

> The size distribution of farms is more equitable than that prevailing in any other state in India. Thus, in Punjab, nearly one-half of the holdings are "medium-sized" (10–30 acres), compared to only an estimated 20 percent of holdings in other Indian states. [Sorkin, 1971, p. 38]

Family planning records indicate that the proportion of couples actively practicing contraception is higher in the Punjab than in any other Indian state.

A noteworthy decline in fertility during the 1960s [in Punjab] appears very probable indeed. [Visaria, 1972, p. 48]

The evidence of agricultural and demographic modernization in Punjab state is reinforced by the Khanna study conducted in a small rural area of Ludhiana district in the late 1950s and again in the late 1960s [Wyon and Gordon, 1971]. Agricultural modernization proceeded rapidly during the 1960s. While crop acreage was about constant from 1960 to 1969, wheat acreage increased from 20 to 40 percent of the total; yields per acre doubled between 1961 and 1968. Crop value increased from 220 to 630 million rupees. Apparently a whole set of dramatic agricultural changes were taking place in the region—all consistent with "development" and "modernization." Aspirations had risen considerably; people were particularly interested in improving housing, in making productive investments (wells, machinery, and so forth), buying land, spending more money on children's marriages, repaying debts, buying cattle, and investing in business [Wyon and Gordon, 1971, pp. 304–308]. Rural fertility has apparently declined since 1959. The estimated crude birth rate declined from 40 per thousand in 1957 to 35 per thousand in 1968, and the proportion of the population less than ten years of age was 15 percent smaller in 1969 than 1959. In one carefully studied village— Narangwal—the crude birth rate fell six points in nine years to 33 per thousand in 1969 [Taylor, 1970, p. 108]. Another indication of socioeconomic and demographic modernization was the rise in female age at marriage from about 17.5 in 1956 to over 20 by 1969. The overall population growth rate increased slightly because the crude death rate had declined from about 17 to 12 (offsetting the decline in the crude birth rate), while net migration out of the community decreased from about 11 per thousand in 1957–1959 to half that in 1968–1969 [Wyon and Gordon, 1971, p. 304]. The authors interpreted the increasing agricultural prosperity as the cause of the slowdown in out-migration. Evidence indicated that the government family planning program was not the cause of preferences for smaller families.

Apparently the chief accomplishment of the programs for family planning had been to induce between one-quarter and one-half of the couples previously practicing birth control to switch to modern methods, easier to use and more effective. [Wyon and Gordon, 1971, p. 298]

In fact, the birth rate declined at a slightly higher rate in the "control population" than in the "test population" (where family planning services were more readily available) during the study period. The authors concluded, however, that

as of 1969 popular response to the family planning program was small, but definite. The program was supplying a felt need with prospects that it likely would grow as more people became conscious of the benefits resting in restriction of family size to numbers they can adequately prepare for a higher standard of living, now within their grasp. [Wyon and Gordon, 1971, p. 314]

This is not to suggest that rural Punjab is characterized by equality in its development. As in most other areas of the low-income world, farmers with smaller holdings seem to be at a relative disadvantage when it comes to obtaining credit and technical advice [Sorkin, 1971, p. 39]. But on balance, agricultural development has apparently been both more rapid and more widely shared in the Punjab than in the rest of India. This suggests that a substantial proportion of the rural population may be experiencing a modernization of their life styles. Associated with these developments has been a decline in overall fertility, which is lacking in other rural areas of India.

Both the Philippines and Thailand are among the group of countries in Tables 3.3 and 4.1 that have less equal income distributions. Evidence suggests that although both countries—especially Thailand—have experienced rather rapid growth in agricultural output, neither country has experienced much rural development as that term has been used in this paper. Until the green revolution of the late 1960s, expansion of agricultural output in both countries was the result of bringing new land under cultivation—that is, farmers simply farmed in the same old ways—rather than due to yield-improving technological innovations. The land ownership pattern is more skewed in both countries than in Taiwan and South Korea. About 40 percent of the cultivators in the Philippines were tenants in 1958, compared with an estimated 20 percent forty years earlier.

The Land Reform Act of 1955 [in the Philippines] created an organization to acquire estate land in excess of 300 hectares (or 600 hectares if held by corporations). . . . Implementation of the act has been further impeded by the high compensation rates paid to landowners, since lands so acquired have often been priced beyond the reach of the occupying tenants. This land reform can be said to have been almost completely ineffectual. [Myrdal, 1968, pp. 1314–1315]

Despite levels of per capita income similar to that of South Korea, fertility remains high in both countries. The crude birth rate in the Philippines has apparently been in the range of 45 to 50 per thousand for the last seventy years and "it has not declined to any important degree within recent years [Concepción, 1970, p. 1].

The overall level of fertility in Thailand has not yet shown evidence of decline from former high levels, and Thai women continue to average about 6.5 births by the time they complete their reproductive years. Certain areas, however, do appear to have declining fertility; and a decline may be setting in for the country as a whole, although available data are not accurate enough to be certain. [Unhanand et al., 1972, p. 3]

At 3.3 to 3.4 percent annually, the population growth rates of both countries are among the highest in the world. Both have recently initiated government-sponsored family planning programs, and in Thailand the program has expanded quite rapidly. About 15 percent of the eligible women in the country were practicing contraception by 1971 [Unhanand et al., 1972, p. 14]. Although this is a large enough proportion of the population to have a dampening effect on overall fertility, the extent of fertility decline, if any, is unknown.

Sri Lanka also is included among the countries in Table 3.3 that have less equal income distributions. Nevertheless, Sri Lanka has experienced considerable fertility decline. The crude birth rate in Sri Lanka is now about 32 per thousand, whereas it was about 40 two decades ago. It appears that the poorest half of the population in Sri Lanka is considerably better off than the poorest half of the population in India, which still has a crude birth rate in the middle 40s, and that the distribution of living conditions is substantially more egalitarian in Sri Lanka than in India. First, Sri Lanka's per capita income is estimated to be about 70 percent higher than that of India. Second, Myrdal [1970, p. 49] believes that Sri Lanka may be the only country in South Asia in which incomes became *more* equally distributed in recent years. Third, Sri Lanka has one of the most effective and comprehensive health systems in the low-income world, and health facilities are extremely well distributed [Myrdal, 1968, chap. 30]. The crude death rate in Sri Lanka is about half that in India. Fourth, Sri Lanka has one of the highest literacy rates in South Asia—about double that of India [Myrdal, 1968]. Fifth, in recent years Sri Lanka has had a program providing two servings of rice daily to the entire population—the first serving free and the second highly subsidized. Finally, although data do not permit a direct comparison, the distribution of land ownership is probably more skewed in India than in Sri Lanka.[12] These and other features of Sri Lanka result in a distribution of levels of living that is considerably more equal than the income distribution alone indicates. Thus, Sri Lanka is not the exception it first appears to be; on the contrary, it is consistent with the central hypothesis of this paper. It is interesting to note, moreover, that Sri Lanka's fertility decline has taken place in the absence of urbanization. From 1946 to 1971, the urban population as a percent of the total population increased by only 1.6 percent, from 20.5 to 22.1 percent [Gunatilleke, 1972, p. 1].

---

[12] Distribution, however, is highly skewed in both countries. Data on India's overall land distribution were given in Chapter 3. In 1962, among paddy farmers in Sri Lanka, 62 percent were full owners, 20 percent were part owners, and 18 percent were full tenants. The latter two groups cultivated 24 percent of the land [Jogaratnam and Schickele, 1970, p. 38]. The land reform provisions of the Paddy Lands Act of 1958, which attempted to control rents and provide more security of occupancy to tenants, have proven very difficult to implement, and the land tenure structure may have worsened since 1962 [Jogaratnam and Schickele, 1970, p. 40]. Nevertheless, the impression is that distribution of land is less skewed in Sri Lanka than in India.

Land-Extensive Agriculture and Fertility Decline

It is clear that in some major regions of the world, agricultural constraints are both qualitatively and quantitatively different from those in Asia. Most of Africa is conventionally viewed as a "land-surplus" region with vast stretches of unexploited but potentially productive land. Hance [1970] has shown the fallacy of this general characterization and has documented the existence of severe land pressures in several critical regions including Burundi, Rwanda, portions of Uganda, Kenya, Malawi, and in some areas of Western Africa in a belt stretching from Senegal to Nigeria. In many of these areas, population densities are among the highest in the world and agricultural production has frequently been unable to keep pace with population growth. One extreme example is a small island in Lake Victoria —Ukara—whose inhabitants had developed prior to European contact a highly intensive system of agricultural cultivation.

> Their methods of husbandry include erosion control, crop rotation, and mixed farming with cultivation of fodder, stabling of the cattle, and use of manure in the fields; their land-tenure system is based on private property, with inheritance and sale of land. The system has been attributed to, and certainly permitted the development of high densities in an insular situation, where no migration was possible. However, it has apparently reached a point where further development is not possible. As far as administrative records and population censuses can be trusted, the Kara have numbered about 16,000 people since the beginning of the century. There has been little, if any growth, whereas administrative records show abundant increase in the rest of the Lake area, where shifting cultivation is still practised. Density is of the order of 620 persons per square mile of area, but only half of the island can be cultivated, and its fertility is low. Excess population moves to the mainland, where labor-intensive techniques are quickly abandoned. [Van de Walle, 1972, pp. 119–120]

In these areas of dense population, lack of modern biological technology is probably a major constraint to rapid growth in agricultural output—as has been the case in Asia. High-yielding varieties of maize have been introduced into Kenya, and a West African regional agricultural research institute has been established in Nigeria for the purpose of developing new high-yielding varieties of food crops. For these regions of dense population, if new biological technologies can be introduced, followed by a relatively equal pattern of agricultural growth and development, sustained fertility reduction may be one of the eventual by-products.

Many other large regions of Africa do not have similar land constraints. Consequently, a more land-extensive form of agriculture—commonly called "slash-and-burn"—is practiced. Typically, after a plot of land has been cultivated for a year or two, the natural fertility of the soil has deteriorated sufficiently so that the cultivators choose to clear a nearby plot by cutting down and burning the foliage; they then farm the new plot until it too must be abandoned. Given a resource endowment that is land abundant, this is a perfectly rational form of agriculture. With some variation it was practiced in the United States during the eighteenth and nineteenth centuries and in Europe in earlier times.

Even under a system of extensive agriculture as found in much of Africa and some areas of Latin America, farmers have been remarkably responsive to new technologies and new economic opportunities. Evidence indicates that there are no unique barriers to agricultural development in Africa, despite the prevalence of views suggesting that African farmers or African ecology are particularly unsuited to agricultural development [Eicher, 1970]. However, the development experiences examined in this paper give very little indication as to whether or not land-abundant agriculture in Africa and elsewhere can be modernized in such a way as to lead to fertility decline, at least in the near future and to the extent experienced in Taiwan and South Korea. In sub-Saharan Africa, fertility rates are high and there has been no evidence of significant fertility decline to date. Van de Walle [1970, p. 255] estimates that crude birth rates are about 48 per thousand in East and West Africa and about 40 per thousand in Central Africa. He believes that particularly in Central Africa, where the relatively lower fertility is largely the consequence of a high incidence of female sterility, fertility will probably *rise* as health conditions improve. Henin [1968, 1969] found that in the Sudan as rural agriculturalists shifted from nomadism to settled farming, their fertility levels increased. While Caldwell [1968] found evidence of fertility decline among the more prosperous urban families in Ghana, and Dow's [1971] data show that in Sierra Leone fertility is somewhat higher in rural than in urban areas, these and other studies have found that in *rural* Africa fertility has not declined and there is little prospect for decline in the near future. Since about 80 percent of Africa's population is estimated to be rural and the rural population is expected to almost double by the year 2000 and still comprise 60 percent of the total (see Tables 2.5 and 2.6), the potential for demographically significant fertility decline in Africa in the near future appears quite limited. Although mortality has continued to decline during the past decade, crude death rates are still generally 20 per thousand or above, about double the rates for Latin America [Heisel, 1971]. There is every possibility that mortality will continue its decline. The prospect, then, is for continued high and perhaps rising rates of population growth in Africa between now and the end of this century.

This chapter has attempted to show that agricultural technologies, development policies, and rural institutions are the key determinants of the process of rural development and, indirectly, rural fertility decline. Appropriate technologies, policies, and institutions can lead to rapid growth in agricultural output and a relatively egalitarian distribution of the benefits of development in rural areas. This can be expected to cause a fairly rapid and widespread process of modernization within rural families, which in turn will lead to a desire for smaller and smaller families and a sustained overall fertility decline. The fertility decline can be considerably enhanced by an effective family planning program. On the other hand, inappropriate technologies, policies, and institutions will probably result in a dualistic pattern of agricultural growth within which a small proportion of the rural population experience rapid improvements in incomes and living conditions and considerable modernization, while living conditions and life styles of most rural families improve little if any. The small but advantaged segment of the rural population may well desire and achieve smaller families but the bulk of the rural families will remain largely traditional with little incentive to have fewer children. Thus, under these conditions there is likely to be little if any decline in overall fertility, and a national family planning program would probably be of little interest to the bulk of the rural population.

Summary and Research Implications

The "Pearson Report" urged an all-out effort to achieve an annual GNP growth rate of 6 percent in the low-income world during the 1970s. Although economic growth rates during the last two decades were not spectacular, GNP grew at an average annual rate of just under 5 percent, which is 1–3 percent higher than during comparable periods in high-income countries. Thus, the record of overall economic growth in and of itself provides little reason for anxiety about prospects for people in the low-income world. On the other hand, population growth rates of 2.5–3 percent annually are discouraging since per capita incomes are therefore rising only half as fast as overall GNP and the per capita income "gap" between high- and low-income countries is increasing.

And, when we examine the available evidence regarding the *distribution* of economic growth and improvements in living conditions and their recent trends and future likelihoods, it becomes obvious that there is cause for alarm. In at least some low-income countries, the well-being of the *poorest* half or more of the population has apparently deteriorated in relative terms and, in some cases, in absolute terms. An initial highly unequal distribution of levels of living has in recent years become even more skewed in many countries. This generalization seems to apply whether one examines employment, incomes, consumption, education, health, or nutrition. With the exception of the small rural landed class, people in rural areas commonly have shared even fewer benefits of economic growth than have urban populations. The inherent urban bias has been aggravated by development policies that have favored the relatively small urban-industrial sector over the much larger rural sector.

While all this is lamentable enough in itself, comparing the experience of several countries suggests that economic growth that is highly distorted and that fails to bring real benefits and more modern life styles to the large bulk of the population cannot be expected to be accompanied by sustained overall fertility decline. Desire for small families is without doubt one aspect of a modern life style, which also includes modern attitudes and tastes regarding consumption, production, and the role of children. There is no basis for hoping that families who are largely traditional in their production and consumption activities will be modern in their fertility behavior. Yet there is virtual unanimity among development specialists that a decline in fertility and population growth rates would provide very substantial benefits to the development process—for both families and society as a whole. These benefits would accrue for almost all the important components of development discussed in this paper—employment, income distribution, education, health, and nutrition.

Rural poverty is self-perpetuating not only because of rapid population growth but also because of institutions and development policies that inhibit greater returns to labor and an improved distribution of incomes. An array of government policies subsidize capital and hold down the growth of employment in both urban and rural areas. Within the rural sector of many countries, the prevailing distribution of land ownership and differential access to credit and supply services further disadvantage the poor and prevent real improvement in their incomes and living conditions. Many economists fear that in the absence of effective reform, existing ownership inequalities will worsen in the years ahead as a consequence of rapid population growth and the incentives produced by the green revolution, which entice landlords to displace tenants so as to capture more of the economic gains.

The net result of these conditions is that the rural poor are denied access to those resources by which they could improve their own incomes and living conditions, break the vicious cycle, and share the fruits of growth. Consequently, their life styles, including their attitudes toward family, children, and fertility behavior, remain largely unchanged.

The discussion in this paper suggests a close complementarity between the goals of (1) rapid growth in agricultural output and food production, (2) a relatively equal participation in and distribution of the benefits of development within the rural sector, and (3) decline in overall fertility and the rate of population growth. Thus, the goal of development must be to achieve a rapid growth in output that is relatively equally distributed. Only when living conditions of the bulk of the rural population are improving rapidly can fertility decline be anticipated.

Much of the analysis in this paper has been based on secondary and often fragmentary data. Thus, although the available evidence seems to be consistent and without significant contradictions, the conclusions and policy implications should be considered no more than tentative. Nevertheless, the relationships analyzed—rural development, improved living conditions, and fertility decline—represent the very core of the development problem in the low-income world, and for this reason, research on the interrelationships analyzed here would appear to be among the most pressing social science research needs in the world today.

Several categories of research can be distinguished. Some are primarily economic in nature. Economic research should attempt to determine how to generate both rapid economic growth and a high degree of equality in its distribution. It is not sufficient to simply discredit the propositions that economic growth is inconsistent with an egalitarian distribution and that eventually development benefits will "trickle down" to the masses. Rather, it is necessary to determine what policy tools are available to effect both growth and a more egalitarian distribution. Some fiscal, employment, public works, educational, health, land tenure, and several other rural development policies have been suggested here. But more work needs to be done to both ascertain the validity of the analyses presented here and elsewhere as well as to determine which policy alternatives are most suitable to various economic, social, and political conditions.

Much more research resources should be directed to actually measuring the distributional aspects of economic growth and development and their trends—incomes, employment, education, health, nutrition, and so on. Our stock of knowledge is meager, in part because of the considerable difficulty and expense such research imposes. But much of the present deficiency is due to the fact that in the past such data were not considered sufficiently important to justify their being gathered. Hopefully the growing concern with the distributional and social justice aspects of development will enhance prospects for more research in this area. Its importance can hardly be overstated.

There are also high-priority population-related categories of research that emerge from this treatment; first, basic demographic research to ascertain what are in fact the prevailing demographic characteristics of populations in the low-income world, what are the trends, and what are the differentials. Remarkable progress has been made in recent years in generating a substantial amount of previously nonexistent basic demographic data, as well as in the development of increasingly sophisticated techniques for analyzing incomplete and inaccurate data. But for large areas of the low-income world, information on current basic demographic characteristics— numbers, age distributions, and fertility and mortality levels—is subject to a wide margin of error, while practically nothing whatsoever is known about trends and differentials.

The social and economic correlates of demographic trends and differentials must be determined. Much more needs to be known about fertility and mortality trends and their differentials in low-income countries, but it is even more crucial to determine the social and economic characteristics of households, communities, and nations, and how these are systematically related to their demographic characteristics. For example, an important hypothesis that could be tested is the following: In traditional settings, increased wealth and health can be expected to lead to short-term *increased* fertility. However, when accompanied by other modernizing forces—education, rapidly rising aspirations, increased consumption of consumer durables, rising aspirations for children—the longer-term effect of rising incomes and levels of living on fertility is fertility *decline*. Asian countries in particular now offer a fascinating laboratory for studying the effects of differential patterns of agricultural development on fertility behavior. For example, fragmentary evidence from the Indian Punjab where dramatic rural modernization is taking place indicates that, compared to other areas in India, fertility is lower and declining and contraceptive practice is higher and rising. Rapid agricultural growth in the Punjab will doubtless continue while other regions more poorly endowed agriculturally will fall farther behind. Comparative longitudinal studies of rural development and fertility change between and within such diverse regions could test the hypothesis that agricultural modernization leads to demographic modernization—that is, fertility decline. Beyond the fragmentary data analyzed in this paper, practically nothing is known about the relationships between the processes of rural development—and particularly its distributional characteristics—and fertility trends and differentials. Research on these relationships could productively be carried out in Africa and Latin America, as well as in Asia.

A final category of priority research would be policy oriented. That is, as information becomes available on demographic trends and differentials and more is known about their social and economic causes and consequences, we need to know what to expect in terms of the impact of specific policy alternatives. A wide range of economic, political, social, and demographic policy alternatives are or could be made available. As for population policies, the options range from simply providing contraceptive information, to subsidized services, to massive programs integrated into ongoing health, education, and rural development activities, to measures "beyond family planning" that would attempt to limit births by economic incentive or legislative fiat. It has been argued in this paper that policies of a non-population nature that are likely to have important demographic consequences include education, health, nutrition, land tenure, employment, fiscal, public works, social services, and urban development. But perhaps even more important, it was also argued that the differential distributional consequences of policy alternatives in each of these fields may have different consequences for fertility, both between various groups or classes in the society and at the overall or aggregate level. Thus, we need much more information on the differential distributional consequences of policy alternatives, and we need to know the impact on demographic variables—and on fertility in particular—of alternative structures of distribution in the development process.

Much of the analysis in this paper was based on cross-sectional data from different countries and regions, although whenever possible time-series data were used relating the process of development to overall fertility levels within an historical context. Research primarily needs to be of the latter form. That is, what is really relevant is the *sequence* of events that interact to produce a given pattern of distribution and fertility behavior.

The evidence currently available on this topic and presented in this monograph, scanty and fragmented though much of it is, basically is consistent and generally supports the analysis and conclusions. But analyses that must rely on highly diffuse and imprecise data and that contain many qualifications and limitations—such as much of the analysis in this paper— are sometimes criticized for being too speculative, even misleading, and for trying to draw strong conclusions from weak evidence. There is probably much validity to such criticisms. But despite these weaknesses and dangers, there is at least one important function that a work such as this can perform. If this monograph serves to stimulate new thinking and new research initiatives on an important but often neglected topic, then it will certainly be justified, even if subsequent research results are at variance with the initial conclusions.

References

Abel, M. E. 1971. *The Distribution of Agricultural Development Gains in India: A Case Study for South and Southeast Asia.* Minneapolis: University of Minnesota, Department of Agricultural and Applied Economics, Staff Paper P71-25.

Abercrombie, K. C. 1969. "Population growth and agricultural development." *Monthly Bulletin of Agricultural Economics and Statistics* 18, no. 4 (April): 1-9.

Adams, D. W. 1970. "Aid agencies and land reform in Latin America: A suggested change in policy." *Land Economics* 46, no. 4 (November): 423-434.

Adelman, I., and Morris, C. T. 1971a. "An anatomy of income distribution patterns in developing nations." *Development Digest* 9, no. 4 (October): 24-37.

―――. 1971b. *Final Report on U.S.A.I.D. Grant scd-2236.* Part I: Summary, Conclusions, and Recommendations; Part III: An Anatomy of Income Distribution in Developing Nations. Washington, D.C.: Office of U.S.A.I.D.

Adulavidhaya, K., and Prachuabmoh, V. 1972. "Some aspects of agricultural production and population growth in Thailand." Paper presented at the Seminar on Effects of Agricultural Innovation in Asia on Population Trends, Manila, February 1972.

Arrighi, G., and Saul, J. S. 1968. "Socialism and economic development in tropical Africa." *Journal of Modern African Studies* 6, no. 2: 141–169.

Barlow, R. 1969. *The Economic Effects of Malaria Eradication.* Ann Arbor: University of Michigan, Bureau of Health Economics, Research Series No. 15.

Becker, G. S. 1960. "An economic analysis of fertility." In National Bureau of Economic Research, *Demographic and Economic Change in Developed Countries,* pp. 209–231. Princeton, N. J.: Princeton University Press.

Beller, I. 1970. "Latin America's unemployment problem." *Monthly Labor Review* 102, no. 5 (November): 3–10.

Belli, P. 1971. "The economic implications of malnutrition: The dismal science revisited." *Economic Development and Cultural Change* 20, no. 1: 1–23.

Berry, R. A. 1970. "Income and wealth distribution in the development process and their relationship to output growth." New Haven, Conn.: Yale University, Economic Growth Center Discussion Paper No. 89.

————. 1972. "Farm size distribution, income distribution, and the efficiency of agricultural production: Colombia." *American Economic Review* 62, no. 2 (May): 403–408.

Borlaug, N. 1971. "The green revolution, peace and humanity." *Population Reference Bureau Selection No. 35* (January).

Boserup, E. 1965. *The Conditions of Agricultural Growth.* Chicago: Aldine.

Brown, L. R. 1963. *Man, Land, and Food: Looking Ahead at World Food Needs.* Washington, D. C.: U. S. Department of Agriculture, Foreign Agricultural Report No. 11.

————. 1965. *Increasing World Food Output.* Washington, D. C.: U. S. Department of Agriculture, Foreign Agricultural Report No. 25.

————. 1968. "New directions in world agriculture." *Studies in Family Planning* 1, no. 32 (June): 1–6.

————. 1970. *Seeds of Change: The Green Revolution and Development in the 1970s.* New York: Praeger.

Byerlee, D. 1971. "Research on migration in Africa: Past, present and future." East Lansing: Michigan State University, Department of Agricultural Economics, Working Paper No. 3a.

————. 1972. "Agricultural development and urban unemployment: A simulation analysis of the Nigerian economy." Ph.D. thesis, Oregon State University.

Byerlee, D., and Eicher, C. K. 1972. "Rural employment, migration, and economic development: Theoretical issues and empirical evidence from Africa." Paper presented at a conference of the International Economics Association, Bad Godesberg, August 1972.

Caldwell, J. C. 1968. *Population Growth and Family Change in Africa: The New Urban Elite in Ghana.* Canberra: Australian National University Press.

Cha, Youn Keun. 1972. "Population trends and family planning program in

Korea." Paper presented at the Seminar on Effects of Agricultural Innovation in Asia on Population Trends, Manila, February 1972.

Christensen, R. P. 1968. *Taiwan's Agricultural Development*. Washington, D. C.: U. S. Department of Agriculture, Foreign Agricultural Economic Report No. 39.

Cleaver, H. M., Jr. 1972. "The contradictions of the green revolution." *Monthly Review* 24, no. 2 (June): 80–111. An abridged version without footnotes is published in *American Economic Review* 62, no. 2 (May 1972): 177–186.

Cline, W. R. 1970. *Economic Consequences of a Land Reform in Brazil*. Amsterdam: North-Holland Publishing Company.

———. 1971. "The potential effect of income redistribution on economic growth in four Latin American countries." *Development Digest* 9, no. 4: 9–23.

Coale, A. J., and Hoover, E. M. 1958. *Population Growth and Economic Development in Low Income Countries*. Princeton, N. J.: Princeton University Press.

Cochrane, W. W. 1969. *The World Food Problem: A Guardedly Optimistic View*. New York: Thomas Y. Crowell.

Concepción, M. B. 1970. "The Philippines." *Country Profiles*. New York: The Population Council (June).

Dalrymple, D. G. 1972. *Imports and Plantings of High-Yielding Varieties of Wheat and Rice in the Less Developed Nations*. Washington, D. C.: U. S. Department of Agriculture, Foreign Economic Development Report 14.

Daly, H. E. 1970. "The population question in northeast Brazil: Its economic and ideological dimensions." *Economic Development and Cultural Change* 18, no. 4 (July): Part 1, 536–574.

———. 1971. "A Marxian-Malthusian view of poverty and development." *Population Studies* 25, no. 1 (March): 25–37.

Dantwala, M. L. 1970. "From stagnation to growth: Relative roles of technology, economic policy and agrarian institutions." *Indian Economic Journal* 18, no. 2 (October–December): 165–192.

Davis, K. 1951. *The Population of India and Pakistan*. Princeton, N. J.: Princeton University Press.

———. 1969. *World Urbanization 1950–1970*. Vol. 1, *Basic Data for Cities, Countries, and Regions*. Berkeley: University of California Press.

Demeny, P. 1971. "The economics of population control." In National Academy of Sciences, *Rapid Population Growth*, pp. 199–221. Baltimore, Md.: Johns Hopkins Press.

Denison, E. F. 1962. *The Sources of Economic Growth in the United States*. Washington, D. C.: Brookings Institution.

de Vries, B. A. 1972. "Unemployment and poverty—what remedies are feasible." *Finance and Development* 9, no. 1 (March): 10–15.

Dorner, P., ed. 1971. *Land Reform in Latin America: Issues and Cases*. Madison: University of Wisconsin Press.

Dorner, P., and Kanel, D. 1971. "The economic case for land reform: Employment, income distribution, and productivity." In *Land Reform in Latin
America: Issues and Cases*, ed. P. Dorner, pp. 41–56. Madison: University
of Wisconsin Press.

Dovring, F. 1970. "Land reform and productivity in Mexico." *Land Economics* 46, no. 3 (August): 264–274.

Dow, T. E., Jr. 1971. "Fertility and family planning in Sierra Leone."
Studies in Family Planning 2, no. 8 (August): 153–165.

Easterlin, R. A. 1969. "Towards a socioeconomic theory of fertility: A survey
of recent research on economic factors in American fertility." In *Fertility
and Family Planning*, eds. S. J. Behrman, L. Corsa, and R. Freedman,
pp. 127–156. Ann Arbor: University of Michigan Press.

Ehrlich, P. 1968. *The Population Bomb*. New York: Ballantine.

Eicher, C. K. 1969. "Production is not sacred." *CERES: FAO Review* 2, no.
3 (May–June): 36–39.

———. 1970. *Research on Agricultural Development in Five English Speaking Countries in West Africa*. New York: Agricultural Development
Council.

Eicher, C. K., and Zalla, T. 1971. "Protein, planners and planning techniques
in Africa." *Rural Africana* 13 (Winter): 50–59.

Eicher, C. K.; Zalla, T.; Kocher, J. E.; and Winch, F. 1970. *Employment
Generation in African Agriculture*. East Lansing: Michigan State University, Institute of International Agriculture, Research Report No. 9.

Enke, S. 1966. "The economic aspects of slowing population growth."
Economic Journal 76, no. 301: 44–56.

———. 1969. "Birth control for economic development." *Science* 164: 798–
802.

Falcon, W. P. 1970. "The green revolution: Generations of problems."
American Journal of Agricultural Economics 52, no. 5 (December):
698–710.

Faundes, A., and Luukkainen, T. 1972. "Health and family planning services
in the Chinese People's Republic." *Studies in Family Planning* 3, no. 7,
supplement (July): 165–176.

Fishlow, A. 1972. "Brazilian size distribution of income." *American Economic
Review* 62, no. 2 (May): 391–402.

Flores, E. 1972. "Latin America: Grim, grim, grim!" *Center Report*. Santa
Barbara, Calif.: Center for the Study of Democratic Institutions (April).

Foland, F. M. 1969. "Agrarian reform in Latin America." *Foreign Affairs*
48, no. 1 (October): 97–112.

Food and Agricultural Organization. 1967. *Production Yearbook*. Rome:
FAO.

———. 1970. *Provisional Indicative World Plan for Agricultural Development*. Rome: FAO.

———. 1971. *Report of the Special Committee on Agrarian Reform*. Rome:
FAO.

Frank, C. R., Jr. 1970. *The Problem of Urban Unemployment in Africa.* Princeton, N. J.: Princeton University, Woodrow Wilson School of Public and International Affairs, Discussion Paper No. 16.

Frederiksen, H. 1969. "Feedbacks in economic and demographic transition." *Science* 166 (November 14): 837–847.

Frejka, T. 1971. "Alternative population growth: World prospects." New York: The Population Council. Mimeographed.

———. 1973. *The Future of Population Growth: Alternative Paths to Equilibrium.* New York: John Wiley and Sons.

Fukutake, T. 1972. "Population and agricultural change in Japan." Paper presented at the Seminar on Effects of Agricultural Innovation in Asia on Population Trends, Manila, February 1972.

Geertz, C. 1963. *Agricultural Involution: The Processes of Ecological Change in Indonesia.* Berkeley: University of California Press.

Ghai, D. P. 1968. "Incomes policy in Kenya: Need, criteria, and machinery." *East African Economic Review* 4, New Series (June): 19–34.

Gotsch, C. H. 1972. "Technical change and the distribution of incomes in rural areas." *American Journal of Agricultural Economics* 54, no. 2 (May): 326–341.

Gunatilleke, G. 1972. "Rural-urban balance and development: The experience of Ceylon." Paper presented at the Seminar on Population and Development, Thailand, June 1972.

Hance, W. A. 1970. *Population, Migration, and Urbanization in Africa.* New York: Columbia University Press.

Hansen, B. 1969. "Employment and wages in rural Egypt." *American Economic Review* 59, no. 3 (June): 298–313.

———. 1971. "Employment and wages in rural Egypt: Reply." *American Economic Review* 61, no. 3 (June): Part 1, 500–508.

Hardee, J. G.; Marzuki, A.; Tan Boon Ann; and Hew Wai Sin. 1972. "Malaysia." *Studies in Family Planning* 3, no. 7 (July): 136–139.

Harmon, A. J. 1970. *Fertility and Economic Behavior in the Philippines.* Santa Monica, Calif.: Rand.

Harris, J. R., and Todaro, M. P. 1970. "Migration, unemployment and development: A two sector analysis." *American Economic Review* 60, no. 1 (March): 126–142.

Hayami, W., and Ruttan, V. W. 1971. *Agricultural Development: An International Perspective.* Baltimore, Md.: Johns Hopkins Press.

Heisel, D. F. 1971. "Population in sub-Saharan Africa: Patterns and prospects." Paper presented to the African Studies Association.

Helleiner, G. K. 1970. "The fiscal role of the marketing boards in Nigerian economic development, 1947–1961." In *Growth and Development of the Nigerian Economy*, eds. C. K. Eicher and C. Liedholm, pp. 119–155. East Lansing: Michigan State University Press. Originally published in *Economics Journal* 74, no. 295 (September 1964): 582–610.

Henin, R. A. 1968. "Fertility differentials in the Sudan." *Population Studies* 22, no. 2 (March): 147–164.

————. 1969. "The patterns and causes of fertility differentials in the Sudan." *Population Studies* 23, no. 2 (July): 171–198.

Hertford, R. 1971. *Sources of Change in Mexican Agricultural Production, 1940–1965.* Washington, D. C.: U. S. Department of Agriculture, Foreign Agricultural Economics Report No. 73.

Hill, G. W. 1964. "The agrarian reform in Costa Rica." *Land Economics* 40, no. 1 (February): 41–48.

Ho, Yhi-Min. 1972. "Development with surplus population—the case of Taiwan: A critique of the classical two-sector model, à la Lewis." *Economic Development and Cultural Change* 20, no. 2 (January): 210–234.

Hooley, R., and Ruttan, V. W. 1969. "The Philippines." In *Agricultural Development in Asia,* ed. R. T. Shank, pp. 215–250. Berkeley: University of California Press.

Hoover, E. M. 1971. "Basic approaches to the study of demographic aspects of economic development: Economic-demographic models." *Population Index* 37, no. 2 (April–June): 66–75.

Hoover, E. M., and Perlman, M. 1966. "Measuring the effects of population control on economic development: A case study of Pakistan." *Pakistan Development Review* 6, no. 4 (Winter): 545–566.

International Labour Organization. 1970. *Towards Full Employment: A Programme for Colombia.* Geneva: ILO.

————. 1971. *Matching Employment Opportunities and Expectations: A Programme of Action for Ceylon.* Geneva: ILO.

————. 1972. *Employment, Incomes and Equality: A Strategy for Increasing Productive Employment in Kenya.* Geneva: ILO.

Jogaratnam, T., and Schickele, R. 1970. "Practical guidelines to agricultural development policies in Ceylon." Peradeniya: University of Ceylon, Agricultural Economics Unit.

Johnson, G. L. 1968. "Food supply, agricultural and economic development." East Lansing: Michigan State University, Consortium for the Study of Nigerian Rural Development, Working Paper No. 8.

Johnson, G. L.; Scoville, O. J.; Dike, G. K.; and Eicher, C. K. 1969. *Strategies and Recommendations for Nigerian Rural Development 1969–1985.* East Lansing: Michigan State University, Consortium for the Study of Nigerian Rural Development.

Johnston, B. F. 1966. "Agriculture and economic development: The relevance of the Japanese experience." *Food Research Institute Studies* 6, no. 3: 215–312.

————. 1970. "Agriculture and structural transformation in developing countries: A survey of research." *Journal of Economic Literature* 8, no. 2 (June): 369–401.

Johnston, B. F., and Cownie, J. 1969. "The seed-fertilizer revolution and labor force absorption." *American Economic Review* 59, no. 3 (September): 569–582.

Johnston, B. F., and Mellor, J. W. 1961. "The role of agriculture in economic development." *American Economic Review* 51, no. 3 (September): 566–593.

Jones, G. W. 1968. "Underutilization of manpower and demographic trends in Latin America." *International Labour Review* 98, no. 5 (November): 451–469.

Kao, C. H. C.; Anschel, K. R.; and Eicher, C. K. 1964. "Disguised unemployment in agriculture: A survey." In *Agriculture in Economic Development*, eds. C. K. Eicher and L. W. Witt, pp. 129–144. New York: McGraw-Hill.

Kasarda, J. D. 1971. "Economic structure and fertility: A comparative analysis." *Demography* 8, no. 3 (August): 307–317.

Keeny, S. M. 1972. "Keeny's Newsletter No. 51." New York: The Population Council (January–February).

Keyfitz, N. 1971. "Changes of birth and death rates and their demographic effects." In National Academy of Sciences, *Rapid Population Growth*, pp. 639–680. Baltimore, Md.: Johns Hopkins Press.

Kim, S. 1971. "Labor migration from the agricultural sector as the source of economic development." Buffalo: State University of New York, Department of Economics, Discussion Paper No. 162.

Kim, Taek Il; Ross, J. A.; and Worth, G. C. 1972. *The Korean National Family Planning Program*. New York: The Population Council.

Kirk, D. 1971. "A new demographic transition?" In National Academy of Sciences, *Rapid Population Growth*, pp. 123–147. Baltimore, Md.: Johns Hopkins Press.

Knight, J. B. 1968. "Earnings, employment, education and income distribution in Uganda." *Bulletin of the Oxford University Institute of Economics and Statistics* 30, no. 4 (November): 167–197.

———. 1971. "Measuring urban-rural income differentials." Paper presented at the Cambridge Employment Conference, September 1971.

Kuznets, Simon. 1955. "Economic growth and income inequality." *American Economic Review* 45, no. 1 (March): 1–28.

———. 1966. *Modern Economic Growth: Rate, Structure, and Spread*. New Haven, Conn.: Yale University Press.

———. 1971. *Economic Growth of Nations: Total Output and Production Structure*. Cambridge, Mass.: Harvard University Press.

———. 1972. "Problems in comparing recent growth rates for developed and less developed countries." *Economic Development and Cultural Change* 20, no. 2 (January): 195–209.

Ladejinsky, W. 1970. "Ironies of India's green revolution." *Foreign Affairs* 48, no. 4 (July): 758–768.

Lee, T. H., and Sun, T. H. 1972. "Agricultural development and population trends in Taiwan." Paper presented to the Seminar on Effects of Agriculture Innovation in Asia on Population Trends, Manila, February 1972.

Leibenstein, H. 1957. *Economic Backwardness and Economic Growth.* New York: Wiley.

————. 1969. "Pitfalls in benefit-cost analysis of birth prevention." *Population Studies* 23, no. 1 (July): 161–170.

Lele, U. J., and Mellor, J. W. 1972. "Jobs, poverty and the 'green revolution.'" *International Affairs* 48, no. 1 (January): 20–32.

Lerner, D. 1968. "Modernization: Social aspects." In *International Encyclopedia of the Social Sciences,* vol. 10, pp. 386–395. New York: Macmillan.

Lewis, J. P. 1971. "The public works approach to low-end poverty programs: The new potentialities of an old answer." Paper submitted for the 1972 meeting of the U. N. Committee on Development Planning, December 1971.

Lewis, W. A. 1966. *Development Planning: The Essentials of Economic Policy.* New York: Harper and Row.

Lindert, P. H. 1971. "Fertility, land, and income distribution: A preliminary macro-model." Madison: University of Wisconsin, Department of Economics. Mimeographed.

Marzuki, A., and Peng, J. Y. 1970. "Malaysia." *Country Profiles.* New York: The Population Council (July).

Mauldin, W. P.; Watson, W. B.; and Noé, L. F. 1970. "KAP surveys and evaluation of family planning programs." New York: The Population Council. Mimeographed.

McNamara, R. S. 1972. "Address to the United Nations Conference on Trade and Development." Washington, D. C.: International Bank for Reconstruction and Development, April 1972.

Meade, J. E. 1967. "Population explosion, the standard of living, and social conflict." *Economic Journal* 77 (June): 233–255.

Miro, C. A., and Mertens, W. 1968. "Influences affecting fertility in urban and rural Latin America." *Milbank Memorial Fund Quarterly* 48, no. 3 (July): Part 2, 89–117.

Mueller, E. 1971. "Agricultural change and fertility change: The case of Taiwan." Ann Arbor: University of Michigan, Department of Economics. Mimeographed.

Myers, R. H. 1969. "Taiwan." In *Agricultural Development in Asia,* ed. R. T. Shand, pp. 25–52. Berkeley: University of California Press.

Myrdal, G. 1968. *Asian Drama: An Inquiry into the Poverty of Nations.* New York: Pantheon.

————. 1970. *The Challenge of World Poverty.* New York: Pantheon.

Nerlove, M., and Schultz, T. P. 1970. *Life and Love Between the Censuses: A Model of Family Decision Making in Puerto Rico.* Santa Monica, Calif.: Rand.

Nicholls, W. H. 1969. "Development in agrarian economies: The role of agricultural surplus, population pressures, and systems of land tenure." In *Subsistence Agriculture and Economic Development,* ed. C. R. Wharton, pp. 296–319. Chicago: Aldine.

————. 1971. "The Brazilian food supply: Problems and prospects." *Economic Development and Cultural Change* 19, no. 3 (April): 378–390.

Orleans, L. A. 1971. "China: Population in the People's Republic." *Population Bulletin* 27, no. 6 (December): 5–37.

Oshima, H. T. 1970. "Income inequality and economic growth: The postwar experience of Asian countries." *Malayan Economic Review* 15, no. 2 (October): 7–41.

————. 1971. "Labor-force 'explosion' and the labor-intensive sector in Asian growth. *Economic Development and Cultural Change* 19, no. 2 (January): 161–183.

Owens, E., and Shaw, R. 1972. *Development Reconsidered.* Lexington, Mass.: Lexington Books.

Paddock, W. C. 1970. "How green is the green revolution?" *Bioscience* 29, no. 16 (August 15): 897–902.

Paddock, W. C., and Paddock, P. 1967. *Famine 1975! America's Decision: Who Will Survive.* Boston: Little, Brown.

Papanek, G. R. 1967. *Pakistan's Development: Social Goals and Private Incentives.* Cambridge: Harvard University Press.

Park, C. H. 1972. "Korean economic development, agricultural innovations, and farm population." Paper presented at the Seminar on Effects of Agricultural Innovation in Asia on Population Trends, Manila, February 1972.

Pearson, L. B. 1969. *Partners in Development.* New York: Praeger.

Perkins, D. H. 1969. *Agricultural Development in China, 1369–1968.* Chicago: Aldine.

Petras, J. F., and LaPorte, R., Jr. 1970. "Modernization from above versus reform from below: U. S. policy toward Latin American agricultural development." *Journal of Development Studies* 6, no. 3 (April): 248–266.

Pokrovsky, A. A. 1970. "Qualitative and quantitative aspects of nutrition." *Impact of Science on Society* 20, no. 3 (July–September): 219–234.

Raj, K. N. 1969. "Some questions concerning growth, transformation and planning of agriculture in developing countries." *Journal of Development Planning* 1: 15–38.

Rangan, K. 1972. "Surplus of grain reported in India." *New York Times,* April 30, p. 4.

Ranis, G. 1968. "Economic growth theory." In *International Encyclopedia of the Social Sciences,* vol. 4, pp. 408–417. New York: Macmillan.

Raulet, H. M. 1970. "Family planning and population control in developing countries." *Demography* 7, no. 2 (May): 211–234.

Rich, W. 1973. *Smaller Families Through Social and Economic Justice.* Washington, D. C.: Overseas Development Council, Monograph No. 7 (January).

Ridker, R. G. 1971. *Employment in South Asia: Problems, Prospects, and Prescriptions.* Washington, D. C.: Overseas Development Council, Occasional Paper No. 1.

Robinson, W. C., and Horlacher, D. E. 1971. "Population growth and economic welfare." *Reports on Population/Family Planning* 6 (February).

Rochin, R. E. 1971. "The impact of dwarf wheats on farmers with small holdings in West Pakistan: Excerpts from recent studies." Islamabad: The Ford Foundation.

Rosenstein-Rodan, P. N. 1961. "International aid for underdeveloped countries." *Review of Economics and Statistics* 43, no. 2 (May): 107–138.

Schluter, M. 1971. *Differential Rates of Adoption of the New Seed Varieties: The Problem of the Small Farm.* Ithaca, N. Y.: Cornell University, Department of Agricultural Economics, Occasional Paper No. 47.

Schultz, T. W. 1964. *Transforming Traditional Agriculture.* New Haven: Yale University Press.

Schultz, T. P. 1969. "An economic model of family planning and fertility." *Journal of Political Economy* 77, no. 2 (March–April): 153–180.

———. 1971. "An economic perspective on population growth." In National Academy of Sciences, *Rapid Population Growth,* pp. 148–174. Baltimore, Md.: Johns Hopkins Press.

———. 1972. "Retrospective evidence of a decline of fertility and child mortality in Bangladesh." *Demography* 9, no. 3 (August): 415–430.

Schultz, T. P., and DaVanzo, J. 1970. *Analysis of Demographic Change in East Pakistan: A Study of Retrospective Survey Data.* Santa Monica, Calif.: Rand.

Seers, D. 1969. "A step towards a political economy of development." *Social and Economic Studies* 18, no. 3 (September): 217–253.

———. 1970. "Challenges to development theories and strategies." In *International Development,* pp. 5–20. Dobbs Ferry, N. Y.: Oceana Publications. Reprinted as "The meaning of development." New York: Agricultural Development Council, September 1970.

Sen, S. R. 1965. "Population, land resources and agricultural growth." *United Nations Population Conference* 3: 409–413. New York: United Nations.

Shaw, R. d'A. 1970. *Jobs and Agricultural Development.* Washington, D. C.: Overseas Development Council, Monograph No. 3.

Silcock, T. H. 1969. "Thailand." In *Agricultural Development in Asia,* ed. R. T. Shand, pp. 103–139. Berkeley: University of California Press.

Simmons, G. B. 1971. *The Indian Investment in Family Planning.* New York: The Population Council.

Singer, H. 1970. "International policies and their effects on employment." Paper presented at the Cambridge Employment Conference, September 1970.

Sorkin, A. L. 1971. "The green revolution." *Growth and Change* 2, no. 3 (July): 36–41.

Starner, F. 1972. "Rice politics in the Philippines." *Far Eastern Economic Review* 75, no. 2 (January 29): 24–25.

Sterba, J. P. 1972. "Asian countries fear a rice glut." *New York Times,* January 16, p. 7.

Stevens, R. D. 1965. *Elasticity of Food Consumption Associated with Changes in Income in Developing Countries.* Washington, D. C.: U. S. Department of Agriculture, Foreign Agricultural Economic Report No. 23.

Taeuber, I. 1958. *The Population of Japan.* Princeton, N. J.: Princeton University Press.

Taiwan Provincial Department of Health. 1971. "Interim Report of Survey and Research Projects Committee on Family Planning, Taiwan." December.

Taylor, C. E. 1970. "Population trends in an Indian village." *Scientific American* (July): 106–113.

Taylor, C. E., and Hall, M.-F. 1967. "Health, population, and economic development." *Science* 157 (August 11): 651–657.

TEMPO. 1968. *Description of the Economic-Demographic Model.* Santa Barbara, Calif.: General Electric Center for Advanced Studies, Document 68TMP-120.

Thiesenhusen, W. C. 1969. "Population growth and agricultural employment in Latin America, with U. S. comparisons." *American Journal of Agricultural Economics* 51, no. 4 (November): 735–752.

———. 1971a. "Latin America's employment problem." *Science* 171 (March 5): 868–874.

———. 1971b. "Technological change and income distribution in Latin American agriculture." Madison: University of Wisconsin, Land Tenure Center Paper No. 78.

———. 1971c. "Employment and Latin American development." In *Land Reform in Latin America: Issues and Cases,* ed. Peter Dorner, pp. 59–76. Madison: University of Wisconsin Press.

Todaro, M. P. 1969. "A model of labor migration and urban unemployment in less developed countries." *American Economic Review* 59, no. 1 (March): 138–148.

———. 1971. "Education and rural-urban migration: Theoretical constructs and empirical evidence from Kenya." Paper prepared for the Conference on Urban Unemployment in Africa, University of Sussex.

Tsu, S. K. 1971. *High-Yielding Varieties of Wheat in Developing Countries.* Washington, D. C.: U. S. Department of Agriculture, Economic Research Service, September.

Tsuchiya, K. 1972. "Population growth and technological progress in Japanese agriculture." Paper presented at the Seminar on Effects of Agricultural Innovation in Asia on Population Trends, Manila, February 1972.

Turnham, D. (assisted by Jaeger, I.) 1971a. *The Employment Problem in Less Developed Countries: A Review of Evidence.* Paris: Organisation for Economic Co-operation and Development, Employment Series No. 1.

———. 1971b. "Income distribution: Measurement and problems." Paper presented at the Conference of the Society for International Development, Ottawa, May 1971.

ul Haq, M. 1971. "Employment and income distribution in the 1970s: A new perspective." *Development Digest* 4, no. 4 (October): 3–8.

Unhanand, M. et al. 1972. "Thailand." *Country Profiles*. New York: The Population Council (March).

United Nations. 1949–1950. *Demographic Yearbook*. New York: United Nations.

––––––. 1951. *Measures for the Economic Development of Underdeveloped Countries*. New York: United Nations, Department of Economic and Social Affairs.

––––––. 1963. *Population Bulletin of the United Nations*, No. 7. New York: United Nations.

––––––. 1965a. *Demographic Yearbook*. New York: United Nations.

––––––. 1965b. *Yearbook of National Account Statistics*. New York: United Nations.

––––––. 1967. *An Analytic Study of the Urban and Rural Population of Costa Rica*. New York: United Nations, Population Division, Working Paper No. 22.

––––––. 1969a. *Growth of the World's Urban and Rural Population, 1920–2000*. New York: United Nations, Department of Economic and Social Affairs, Population Studies No. 44.

––––––. 1969b. *Demographic Yearbook*. New York: United Nations.

––––––. 1970. *Demographic Yearbook*. New York: United Nations.

––––––. 1971. *A Concise Summary of the World Population Situation in 1970*. New York: United Nations, Department of Economic and Social Affairs, Population Studies No. 48.

United States. 1960. *Historical Statistics of the United States: Colonial Times to 1957*. Washington, D. C.: U. S. Department of Commerce, Bureau of the Census.

––––––. 1970. *Area Handbook for Costa Rica*. Washington, D. C.: U. S. Department of State.

van de Walle, E. 1970. "The population of tropical Africa in the 1980s." In *Africa in the Seventies and Eighties: Issues in Development*, ed. F. S. Arkhurst, pp. 247–271. New York: Praeger.

––––––. 1972. "Implications of increases in rural density." In *Population Growth and Economic Development in Africa*, ed. S. H. Ominde and C. N. Ejiogu, pp. 117–122. London: Heinemann.

Visaria, P. 1972. "The adoption of innovations in agriculture and population trends in India." Paper presented at the Seminar on Effects of Agricultural Innovation in Asia on Population Trends, Manila, February 1972.

Weisskoff, R. 1970. "Income distribution and economic growth in Puerto Rico, Argentina, and Mexico." New Haven, Conn.: Yale University, Economic Growth Center Discussion Paper No. 93.

Wharton, C. R., Jr. 1969. "The green revolution: Cornucopia or Pandora's box." *Foreign Affairs* 47, no. 3 (April): 464–476.

World Bank (International Bank for Reconstruction and Development). 1971. *World Bank Atlas, 1971.*

Worth, G.; Watson, W. B.; Dae Woo Han; Finnigan, O. D.; and Keeny, S. M. 1971. "Korea/Taiwan 1970: Report on the national family planning programs." *Studies in Family Planning* 2, no. 3 (March): 57–69.

Wyon, J. B., and Gordon, J. E. 1971. *The Khanna Study: Population Problems in the Rural Punjab.* Cambridge, Mass.: Harvard University Press.

Yale Economic Growth Center. 1971. "A summary of recent findings of Economic Growth Center research." New Haven, Conn.: Yale University. Mimeographed.

Yudelman, M.; Butler, G.; and Banerji, R. 1971. *Technological Change in Agriculture and Employment in Developing Countries.* Paris: Organisation for Economic Co-operation and Development, Employment Series No. 4.